MUTINY
on the
BOUNTY

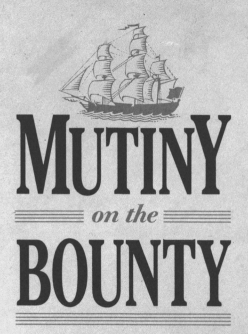

MUTINY
on the
BOUNTY

The Story of
Captain William Bligh seaman, navigator, surveyor
and of the Bounty mutineers

STATE LIBRARY
OF NEW SOUTH WALES

ACKNOWLEDGEMENTS

Previous page
Robert Dodd. The
Mutineers turning Lieut.
Bligh and part of the
Officers and Crew adrift
from His Majesty's Ship the
Bounty, *1790. SLNSW*
(No.33)

The rations and other
resources allowed Bligh and
his men by the mutineers
were minimal, and it was
only just prior to their being
cast adrift that Fletcher
Christian allowed some
clothing, salt pork, and four
cutlasses to be thrown down
to them.

Mutiny on the Bounty was curated by Elizabeth Egan, with curatorial assistance from Paul Brunton, Elizabeth Imashev, John Murphy and Di Rhodes. Grateful acknowledgement is made to the curatorial team and Richard Ormond, Ron Coleman, Glynn Christian and Gavin Kennedy for their contributions to the catalogue.

Acknowledgement is also made to Anne Robertson who coordinated the editing and production of the catalogue, Kerry Sullivan and Christine Pryke for coordination assistance, the State Library's Volunteers for proofreading assistance and Ellen Cominsky, Malcolm McLeod and Maree Jenner of the Library's photographic service, Images Now, for photography of the Library's material for the catalogue.

The Library's gratitude is extended to a number of individuals and institutions for generously lending material to the exhibition. These include: Berkelouw Book Dealers, Berrima; National Library of Australia, Canberra; the National Maritime Museum, Greenwich; Public Record Office, London and the Queensland Museum, Brisbane.

The exhibition has been coordinated by Maisy Stapleton (to August 1990) and Sally Gray (from September 1990) and designed by Phil Verner and the Library Design Studio. Helen Kon coordinated the education programme with the assistance of the Library's Education Branch and Volunteers. Public Relations has been organised by Janette Parkinson, Gill Cavenagh and Diana Calleja. Jo McIntyre, Margy Burn and Rosemary Block have been of assistance in developing the exhibition. The Library's Preservation Branch under the management of Allan Howell and Avryl Whitnall has undertaken the conservations of many of the items on display. Grateful acknowledgement is made to the many other members of the Library's staff who have assisted in the development and operation of the exhibition.

Many individuals have also assisted with the exhibition including Jennifer Cox, Desmond Freeman, David McNicoll, Norfolk Island Radio Station, Bill Shanahan, Sotheby's London, Robert Varman and Stephen Walters.

SSB advertising has provided creative services for the advertising campaign and thanks are extended to David Sherbon, Simon Connelly and Mike Preston.

Qantas is gratefully acknowledged for their sponsorship of air freight of material from London.

Published by the State Library of New South Wales 1991

Mutiny on the Bounty: the story of Captain William Bligh seaman, navigator, surveyor and of the Bounty mutineers.

Bibliography.
ISBN 0 7305 7986 7.

1. Bligh, William, 1754-1817. 2. Christian, Fletcher, 1764-1793. 3. Bounty (Ship). 4. Bounty Mutiny, 1789, I. State Library of New South Wales.

910.45

Designed by Christie & Eckermann Art & Design Studio, Sydney

Typeset by Authotype Photosetters Pty Ltd, Sydney

Printed by Kyodo Printing Co. Ltd.

CONTENTS

Bligh's signet ring, private seal and wax impression from seal. SLNSW (No.102, 103)

These relics were originally in the collection of William Russell Bligh, grandson of William Bligh and were purchased by Sir William Dixson in 1939.

In later years William Bligh used the coat of arms of the Earls of Darnley. William was named after the father of John Bligh, first Earl of Darnley. The ring displays the motto Finem Respice (Consider the end).

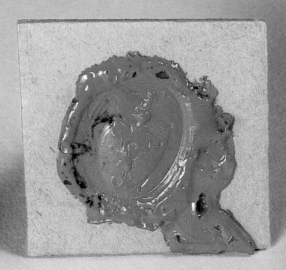

FOREWORD

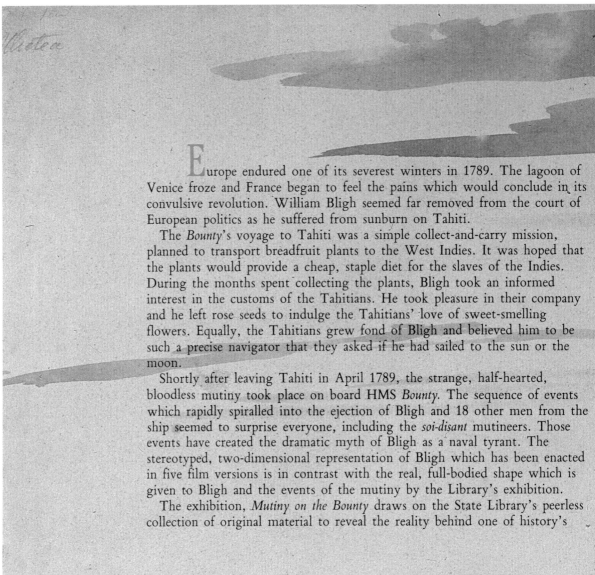

Europe endured one of its severest winters in 1789. The lagoon of Venice froze and France began to feel the pains which would conclude in its convulsive revolution. William Bligh seemed far removed from the court of European politics as he suffered from sunburn on Tahiti.

The *Bounty*'s voyage to Tahiti was a simple collect-and-carry mission, planned to transport breadfruit plants to the West Indies. It was hoped that the plants would provide a cheap, staple diet for the slaves of the Indies. During the months spent collecting the plants, Bligh took an informed interest in the customs of the Tahitians. He took pleasure in their company and he left rose seeds to indulge the Tahitians' love of sweet-smelling flowers. Equally, the Tahitians grew fond of Bligh and believed him to be such a precise navigator that they asked if he had sailed to the sun or the moon.

Shortly after leaving Tahiti in April 1789, the strange, half-hearted, bloodless mutiny took place on board HMS *Bounty*. The sequence of events which rapidly spiralled into the ejection of Bligh and 18 other men from the ship seemed to surprise everyone, including the *soi-disant* mutineers. Those events have created the dramatic myth of Bligh as a naval tyrant. The stereotyped, two-dimensional representation of Bligh which has been enacted in five film versions is in contrast with the real, full-bodied shape which is given to Bligh and the events of the mutiny by the Library's exhibition.

The exhibition, *Mutiny on the Bounty* draws on the State Library's peerless collection of original material to reveal the reality behind one of history's

N 23

most frequently distorted episodes. In an era of mass reproduction and instant multiple copies it is particularly haunting to be placed in contact with the unique, original artefacts, paintings, sketches, manuscripts, maps and publications of the period. Within its Mitchell and Dixson collections, the State Library holds the largest and most valuable collection of Bligh material, unrivalled throughout the world. Most of the items which form these collections enjoy an impeccable provenance as they were presented to the Library by direct descendants of William Bligh.

For some time libraries have been progressive and innovative in the development and application of computer technology. Through computer networks they have made current, complex information accessible across vast distances. In the same spirit of cooperation it has been possible to complement the Library's exhibition items with important material held both in private hands and in institutions, both in Australia and overseas. The Library's gratitude is extended to these individuals, and to the National Maritime Museum, Greenwich, the Public Record Office, London, the National Library of Australia, Canberra and the Queensland Museum, Brisbane. Through their generosity, visitors to the exhibition can witness as complete an evaluation of Bligh's career as the surviving documents allow.

Alison Crook
State Librarian

Henry Roberts. Ulietea, one of the Society Islands, 1773? SLNSW (No.1)

INTRODUCTION

William Bligh was born in Plymouth, England on 9 September 1754, and joined the Royal Navy on 27 July 1770. Bligh's first major appointment was on James Cook's third and last voyage, during which he served as master of HMS *Resolution* (1776-1779).

Bligh admired Cook and learnt much from him about naval management. He was critical of the behaviour of some of his fellow officers at the time of the attack on Cook by the Hawaiians. The official account of the voyage, completed by Lieutenant James King for the Admiralty, contained no mention of the culpability of some of Cook's officers in the affair, and Bligh felt his work on the surveys and charts was not sufficiently acknowledged in it.

On 4 February 1781, William Bligh married Elizabeth Betham at the Onchan Parish Church near Douglas in the Isle of Man. It was to prove a very happy marriage. Elizabeth was from a rich and influential family. Her father, Richard Betham of Thrimby Grange, Westmoreland, was the collector of customs at Douglas. Dr Neil Campbell, her maternal grandfather, was Chaplain to the King and the Principal of Glasgow University. Elizabeth's uncle, Duncan Campbell, was a wealthy and successful merchant, who owned several merchant ships plying the West Indies routes and acted as the shipping contractor to the Royal Navy.

Bligh's naval career prospered. He was rewarded with the rank of Lieutenant on 5 August 1781 after participating in the action at Dogger Bank and later took part in the relief of Gibraltar, 13 October 1782. With the declaration of peace on 13 January 1783, Bligh was placed on half pay.

On the advice of Duncan Campbell, Bligh sought written clearance from the Admiralty to enter the merchant service. In July 1783 Bligh embarked on a mercantile career. From 1783 to 1787 Bligh acted as Campbell's agent in Jamaica and commanded a series of merchant ships, the *Lynx, Cambrian* and in 1787 the *Britannia*. Midshipman Fletcher Christian volunteered for service with Bligh and sailed with him in the *Britannia*. Bligh arrived back in England on 5 August 1787 to find he had been appointed to command a vessel taking part in a joint expedition to the South Seas organized by Sir Joseph Banks and the Admiralty. The purpose of the expedition was to collect breadfruit plants from Tahiti for transplantation in the West Indies. The plants were to provide a cheap food for slaves.

FITTING OUT FOR A VOYAGE TO THE SOUTH SEAS

By 5 May 1787 the British Government had framed instructions for an expedition to collect and convey commercial plant species, including the

breadfruit of Tahiti and the mangostanan *(magosteen Garcinia mangostana)* from Java, to the West Indies under the direction of Sir Joseph Banks. The Admiralty opened tenders for the purchase of a suitable ship, to be refitted for the voyage under Banks' instructions at the Deptford Yard. A 91 feet (27.7 metres) long merchant ship weighing only 215 tons, the *Bethia,* was purchased for 1,960 pounds sterling. The *Bethia* was smaller than HMS *Endeavour,* considered a small ship at 368 tons. Renamed HMS *Bounty,* she left the dockyard equipped with a copper sheathed hull to guard against the marine worm, *Teredo navalis,* four 4pdr guns, ten swivel guns and fittings suited to her naval and botanical purpose. Bligh describes the ship's figurehead as 'a pretty Figure Head of a Woman in a Riding Habit'.

Lieutenant William Bligh was commissioned on 16 August 1787. Bligh's experience made him the ideal candidate. The small size of the *Bounty* led to crowding and to the inadequate manning of the expedition. The absence of marines, to act as the ship's police, was a considerable risk when the commander was the only commissioned officer on board. Bligh was refused the rank of post captain, possibly because the Admiralty viewed the enterprise as a botanical collect-and-carry mission of little importance.

THE FIRST BREADFRUIT VOYAGE IN HMS BOUNTY

HMS *Bounty* left Spithead for the English Channel on 23 December 1787. Bligh's orders were to approach Tahiti from Cape Horn and to return to England via the Cape of Good Hope and the British West Indies. A delayed departure meant that Bligh would be sailing the Horn route late in the season, a time of notoriously harsh weather. After several vain attempts to round the Horn in the face of snow storms, constant rain, cold gales and

Above left

John Russell. Captain William Bligh R.N., 1791. Courtesy Sotheby's (London)

The most famous portrait of Bligh, done on his return from the First Breadfruit Voyage, at the time he was facing charges for the Mutiny on the Bounty.

Above right

John Russell. Elizabeth Bligh, 1802. Courtesy Sotheby's (London)

A charming portrait in pastels, showing Elizabeth Bligh a few years before William was asked to become Governor of New South Wales. Elizabeth did not accompany him, but stayed with five of their six daughters in England because of ill-health.

William Hodges. View of Part of Oaitepeha Bay in the Islands of Otahiti, 1773. Kindly lent by the National Maritime Museum, London

Below

Thomas Gosse. Transplanting of the Bread-fruit-trees from Otaheite, 1796. SLNSW (No.123)

The two men in shirtsleeves loading the young breadfruit are presumably the botanists, James Wiles and Christopher Smith. Looking on are Bligh in the ship's boat and King Pomare I of Tahiti.

high seas, Bligh admitted defeat on 22 April 1788 and turned the
Bounty for the Cape of Good Hope and Tahiti. HMS *Bounty* finally
anchored in Matavai Bay, Tahiti, on 26 October 1788.

The collection of breadfruit plants took five months. After
the privations of the voyage, the ship's company welcomed the
chance to relax in this tropical paradise with its beautiful and
welcoming women, exotic customs and delicious fresh food.
Paintings by Webber and others show Tahiti as it appeared
to the European eye.

THE MUTINY

The *Bountry* left Tahiti on 4 April 1789. On 28 April 1789, 10 leagues
(55 kilometres) from Tofoa, some of the ship's crew mutinied, led by
Fletcher Christian. Bligh and 18 loyal crew members were cast adrift in
the *Bounty*'s launch, a 23 feet (7 metres) longboat. None of the 19
men in the open boat were to see either Fletcher Christian or HMS
Bounty again.

Bligh made for Tofoa to take on supplies of food and water. Here on 3
May 1789, they were attacked by unfriendly natives and John Norton was
killed trying to free the launch's shore line for a hurried escape. After some
deliberation, Bligh decided to head for the Dutch settlement at Timor.

Solanum viride, *engraving
from the* Banks
Florilegium *(Alecto
Historical Editions, London,
1988) from the original
drawing by Sydney
Parkinson. SLNSW
(No.10)*

*Engraved from one of the
thousands of original
drawings done on Cook's
First Voyage by Sydney
Parkinson for Sir Joseph
Banks. This plant from the
Society Islands which include
Tahiti, is related to the
breadfruit species, native to
the Islands. It was thought
that breadfruit could prove a
cheap and reliable food
source for slaves in the
West Indies, if transplanted
there.*

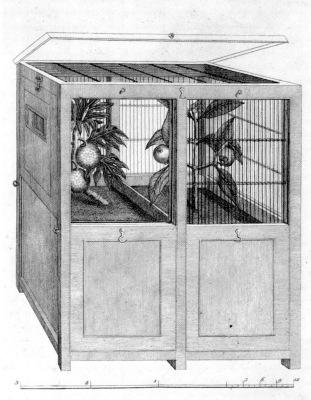

John Ellis. A Description
of the Mangostan and the
Breadfruit *(1775).
Reproduction of engraving.
SLNSW
(No.13)*

*The book includes practical
advice for transportation of
the plants from The Pacific.
In the early 1770s, West
Indian plantation owners
enthusiastically supported the
idea of the breadfruit to
provide cheap food for their
slaves.*

A Wired Case for bringing over the Bread Fruit Tree; the Mangostan
or any other usefull Plants from East India or the South Seas.

Published as the Act directs Nov.r 29.th 1774 by I. Ellis Grays Inn London.

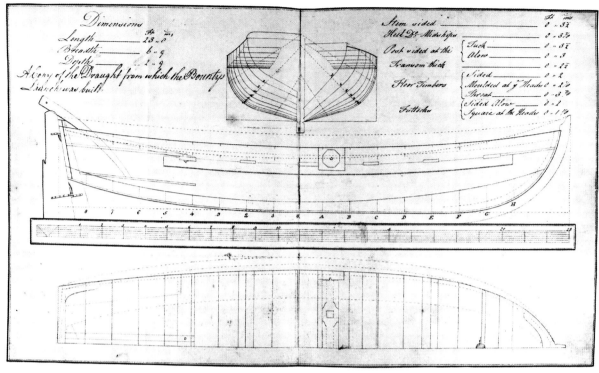

Above
Original drawing of the Bounty's launch. The sturdy design of the launch, with its strong, leak-proof hull, proved equal to the rigours of Bligh's 3,618 nautical mile (6,705km) voyage, from Tofoa outside Tahiti to Coupang, Timor. Submersion was an undeniable hazard for an overloaded boat sitting low in the water. The crew bailed constantly throughout the voyage.
SLNSW (No. 36)

Left
The original manuscript logbooks kept by William Bligh on HMS Bounty. These are Bligh's private logbooks from which the official copies were made. They were donated to the Library in 1902 by Bligh's grandson, W.R. Bligh.
SLNSW (No. 27)

'These Views I took the morning after I landed on Restoration Island' from the private log of William Bligh.
Bligh sailed 3,618 nautical miles (6,705km) from the scene of the mutiny outside Tahiti to Timor in an open, seven metre launch.
A sketch of the launch by Bligh can be seen in the bottom left-hand corner.
SLNSW (No.27)

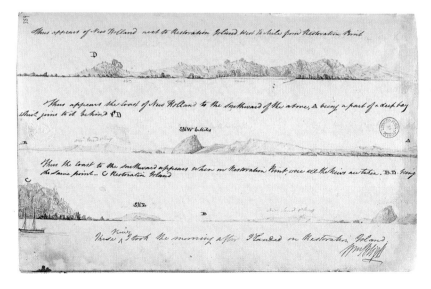

The launch sailed through the Fiji islands, where it out ran two hostile sailing canoes and through the Great Barrier Reef, off the coast of Queensland, to make landfall at Restoration Island, named by Bligh for the anniversary of the Restoration of King Charles II and for replenishing their dwindling food stocks. On 12 June 1789, after 41 days at sea and sailing 6,705 kilometres the island of Timor was sighted by the *Bounty*'s launch. At daylight on 14 June 1789, the boat entered Coupang harbour and the boat's crew was invited to land by the Dutch authorities. Here Bligh made a formal statement to the Dutch authorities about the mutiny and the circumstances of his arrival in Coupang and provided them with a descriptive list of the mutineers. After the men's health had improved, Bligh purchased a Dutch schooner, which he named the *Resource* and with the *Bounty*'s launch in tow sailed on 20 August 1789, for Batavia (Jakarta), the capital of the Dutch East Indies, and the promise of a passage on a Dutch packet bound for Europe. Bligh, accompanied by John Samuel his clerk and his servant John Smith, left Batavia on 16 October 1789 in the Dutch Packet *Vlydte,* reaching Portsmouth 13 March 1790.

The remaining men were left behind in Batavia to make their way back to England as ship's passages became available. Only 11 lived to return to England. Their survival was entirely owing to Bligh's seamanship and judicious command.

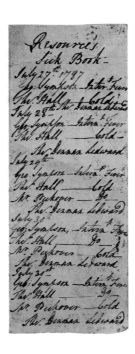

'Resources Sick Book'. At Coupang Bligh purchased a Dutch schooner, which he named Resource, and sailed to Batavia, the capital of the Dutch East Indies. In this notebook Bligh logs the health of his crew. The fact that he misdates the year perhaps indicates his own fatigued condition.
SLNSW (No. 29)

HMS PANDORA IN PURSUIT OF THE MUTINEERS

After Captain Bligh with 18 others were cast adrift in the launch Fletcher Christian sailed off in HMS *Bounty* with a crew of 24. On 24 May 1789, she stopped briefly at Tubuai, an island discovered by Cook in 1777. After some skirmishes with the natives the *Bounty* left for Tahiti where she picked up supplies, and a Tahitian complement of nine women, eight men, ten boys and several stowaways. The *Bounty* then returned to Tubuai where Fletcher Christian hoped to establish a settlement. This proved a failure and the *Bounty* returned to Tahiti in September 1789 where 16 of the mutineers elected to remain.

The *Bounty* then sailed from Tahiti on 23 September 1789 for Pitcairn Island. On 24 March 1791 the surviving mutineers on Tahiti were arrested by Captain Edward Edwards of the 24 gun frigate HMS *Pandora* on Admiralty orders. Edwards then continued the search among the islands for the *Bounty* and Fletcher Christian's mutineers without success. On 28 August 1791, HMS *Pandora* struck and foundered on the Great Barrier Reef. She sank with the loss of 31 crew and four of the mutineers who had been incarcerated in 'Pandora's Box', the ship's prison cell on the quarter deck. The survivors arrived back in England on 18 June 1792 and were imprisoned in HMS *Hector* to await court-martial for mutiny.

COURT-MARTIAL OF THE BOUNTY MUTINEERS

The court-martial of the mutineers was held from 12 September 1792 to 18 September 1792, on board HMS *Duke.* Lord Hood, Commander-in-Chief of the fleet at Spithead, presided over a bench composed of 11 post captains. Ten men stood trial.

At this time, Bligh had left England on his second breadfruit voyage. His written evidence exonerated four crew members, Thomas McIntosh, Joseph Coleman, Charles Norman and Michael Byrne, who had remained on board HMS *Bounty* because there was no room in the launch. Thomas Ellison,

Thomas Burkitt and John Millward were hanged from the yardarm of HMS *Brunswick* on 29 October 1792. James Morrison and Peter Heywood were found guilty but later pardoned and William Musprat was released on a technicality.

The court-martial and its aftermath served to undermine Bligh's reputation in some naval circles. The evidence for the defence presented by Morrison, Heywood and Edward Christian, Fletcher's brother, questioned Bligh's ability to command and the truth of his public writings concerning the mutiny.

THE HISTORY OF THE PITCAIRNERS

Early on the morning of 23 September 1789, Fletcher Christian, Edward Young, Alexander Smith, William McCoy, Matthew Quintal, John Williams, Isaac Martin, John Mills and William Brown sailed from Tahiti in HMS *Bounty,* kidnapping six Polynesian men, 19 Polynesian women and a young female child, Sully. Six of the older women were released at Moorea and Christian and his companions sailed in search of an island that was uninhabited and well out of the usual shipping routes.

The *Bounty* is thought to have covered some 8,000 miles (14,826 kilometres) before reaching Pitcairn Island on 15 January 1790. A publication by the island's discover, Philip Carteret, is known to have been on board HMS *Bounty*. A navigational error made by Carteret meant that this small island remained lost to shipping and gave the mutineers and their party a concealed refuge. Their secret remained secure until Captain Mayhew Folger in the American whaling ship *Topaz* of Boston rediscovered the island by chance in 1808.

Shortly after her arrival at Pitcairn Island, the *Bounty* caught fire in Bounty Bay on 23 January 1790. Matthew Quintal is credited with setting her alight, overcome with the fear of discovery and certain retribution by the Royal Navy.

The community Folger found living on Pitcairn Island in 1808 consisted of four Tahitian women and their children living under the pastoral care of Alexander Smith, the only surviving *Bounty* mutineer. Life on Pitcairn Island had proved unstable and violent in the early years. There was conflict between the Europeans and the Tahitians who had accompanied them, and several men were murdered. All but one of the mutineers, Edward Young, died an unnatural death. Alexander Smith, the only extant mutineer, succumbed to alcohol.

In 1814 HMS *Briton* and *Tagus* under Sir Thomas Staines and Captain P. Pipon called at the island. Their report to the Admiralty emphasized the piety of John Adams (who enlisted on the *Bounty*'s muster roll under the alias of Alexander Smith) and commended the settlement to the English Missionary Society. These visits to Pitcairn Island caused a sensation in the press and writings on Pitcairn topics, as well as visits to the island, became common. Discrepancies in the stories told by John Adams to the different visitors fuelled the myths associated with the establishment of the settlement on the island. The true circumstances surrounding the death of Fletcher Christian were deliberately obscured by John Adams and have been the cause of much continuing speculation. Despite his fears, Adams never stood trial for mutiny. He died on 5 March 1829.

BLIGH'S SECOND BREADFRUIT VOYAGE IN HMS PROVIDENCE AND THE TENDER ASSISTANT, 1791-1793

Despite the failure of the *Bounty* mission, Sir Joseph Banks continued to press George III and the Admiralty for a second expedition to transport breadfruit from Tahiti to the West Indies, with Bligh in command. On 3 August 1791 William Bligh, now a post captain, returned to the Pacific with a well equipped expedition to complete this aim. The manning of the expedition, the size of the two ships chosen and their provisioning were the direct result of Bligh's experiences on the *Bounty* voyage.

The expedition returned to England on 7 August 1793 after a successful voyage. The breadfruit and other exotic plants were transplanted to Jamaica, St Vincent and St Helena, and a complement was brought back to His Majesty's Botanic Garden at Kew. In addition, Bligh and his officers had carried out important hydrographic surveys of the Fiji Islands and Torres Strait.

Shortly after Bligh's return home the Royal Society awarded him its Gold Medal and elected him F.R.S. (Fellow of the Royal Society) in 1801. Public acclaim for the success of the expedition went to the organizer Sir Joseph Banks rather than Bligh. Bligh had lost the favour of the Admiralty, as a result of growing hostility towards him in some naval circles, incited by the influential friends and relatives of two *Bounty* mutineers, Peter Heywood and Fletcher Christian.

Little is known of this successful voyage as Bligh did not publish an account. Before he sailed for New South Wales in 1806 he prepared a portfolio of charts and drawings for inclusion in a prospective publication. This collection was left with his wife Elizabeth in England but was not used.

The breadfruit plants successfully adapted to their new habitat in the West Indies although the fruit initially proved unpalatable to the slaves who preferred their native plantains. Today breadfruit has become an integral part in the diet of West Indians and is often a staple in rural areas when in season.

Bligh received a number of commands following the voyage of the *Providence,* and fought with distinction in the battles of Camperdown (1797) and Copenhagen (1801).

George Tobin. The Bread Fruit of Otahytey, 1792. SLNSW (No. 118)

George Tobin. West side of Port Morant, Jamaica . . . 1793, SLNSW (No.118)

Marc Clark, sculptor. Maquette for statue of William Bligh, 1986. Kindly lent by David McNicoll, Sydney (No.80)

The model for the statue of William Bligh erected in 1987 at Circular Quay West, Sydney, adjacent to Cadman's Cottage. It is the only statue of Bligh in Sydney and pays tribute to his time in New South Wales (1806-1808).

GOVERNOR BLIGH IN NEW SOUTH WALES

In March 1805, Lord Camden invited Sir Joseph Banks to consider possible names for nomination as the new Captain General and Governor-in-Chief of the Territory of New South Wales and its Dependencies.

Banks offered the post to William Bligh. Bligh, then a post captain, decided to accept, although it meant leaving active sea duty with its promise of speedy promotions and his wife Elizabeth, who was too ill to attempt the journey.

Bligh, newly promoted to Commodore, left for New South Wales in February 1806 on board the transport *Lady Madeleine Sinclair,* one of a convoy of ships. They were escorted by HMS *Porpoise* commanded by Captain Joseph Short. Bligh was accompanied by his daughter Mary and her husband Lieutenant John Putland, who was to act as Bligh's aide-de-camp in New South Wales.

The convoy arrived in Port Jackson on 6 August 1806 and Bligh transferred to HMS *Porpoise* to receive the formal welcome as the new Governor.

Before leaving his post as Governor, King granted land to Bligh, 240 acres (97 hectares) at Sydney, 105 acres (42 hectares) at Parramatta and 100 acres (40 hectares) at Rouse Hill on the Hawkesbury road. On assuming the Governorship, Bligh assigned 790 acres (320 hectares) to Mrs King, and 600 acres (243 hectares) to the Putlands.

Bligh's reforms, designed to help small holders, antagonized the leading men of the colony, notably John Macarthur with whom he was soon in dispute. His scathing attitude to the military, possibly partly fuelled by inter-disciplinary rivalry, offended the soldiers and turned them into his enemies. On the evening of 26 January 1806, having been called on by John Macarthur and others to arrest Governor Bligh and declare martial law, Major George Johnston, at the head of the New South Wales Corps, marched up Bridge Street from the barracks, arrested Governor Bligh and assumed control of the colony.

On 31 July 1811, four weeks after Johnston's trial, Bligh was gazetted Rear-Admiral of the Blue Squadron, back dated to July 1810. He was later promoted to Rear-Admiral of the White Squadron in 1812 and in 1814 to Vice-Admiral of the Blue. From time to time he acted as an adviser to the Admiralty but did not again take command of a ship.

After the death of Bligh's wife on 15 April 1812 Bligh and his unmarried daughters moved from London to a Kentish manor house at Faringdon, near Maidstone. Bligh collapsed and died on 7 December 1817, while on a visit to London. He was buried next to his wife in St Mary's Churchyard, Lambeth.

Elizabeth Egan

WILLIAM BLIGH'S ROYAL NAVY

Richard Ormond

Artist unknown. Miniature portrait of William Bligh, 1814? SLNSW (No.84)
Painted when Bligh was 60 years old, after he had successfully defended his stand in New South Wales. He is shown in the uniform of a Vice-Admiral. The miniature originally belonged to Bligh's daughter, Elizabeth, and was purchased from a descendant in 1936.

Mutiny on the *Bounty* is significant on three counts. First, as a confrontation between personalities and principles quite unique in the annals of the Navy; second, for the heroic consequences that followed on from the act of mutiny itself, in particular Bligh's open boat crossing (he sailed from Tofoa across the Pacific to Australia and entered the Timor Sea), and the establishment of the Pitcairn settlement; and finally for the light which the mutiny casts on the role of the Navy in the field of exploration and navigation.

The idea of mutiny appeals to the popular imagination, and most people assume it was a fairly common occurrence. In the Navy it was not. There were plenty of incidents that went by the names of mutiny during the 18th century; refusals to go to sea, occupation of ships and so on, but these were lower deck protests against pay and conditions. Seizing one of His Majesty's ships on the high seas and casting the captain adrift was an event almost without precedent. It explains the rapidity with which the Admiralty responded by dispatching a warship to bring the mutineers to justice. Such an act of flagrant disobedience struck at the very foundations of law and order on which the Navy was built. The mutiny would never have taken place had it not been led by someone as senior as Fletcher Christian, for it required qualities of leadership to effect it. Interest in the mutiny has focused on the personal confrontation between Captain William Bligh and Mr Fletcher Christian, his second in command. The increasingly tense and confrontational atmosphere on board ship, after the long stay in Tahiti, brought out the worst in both men, overbearing and bullying characteristics in Bligh, as he struggled to assert authority; suicidal tendencies in Christian. That this drama was played out on an overcrowded ship, many thousands of miles from home, and cut off for more than a year from European contacts, underlines its sensational aspects. In the unlikely event of such a happening in home waters, it would have been a tame event by comparison: no fierce gales around Cape Horn; no exotic Pacific paradise; no breadfruit; no danger in unknown seas; no aberrant psychological behaviour brought on by stress and confinement.

At the heart of the mutiny lies the issue of whether it was justified. It is no coincidence that its bicentenary coincided with that of the French Revolution. This was the age of Jean Jacques Rousseau, Tom Paine and *The Rights of Man*. Can the overthrow of a tyrannical authority be justified by an appeal to natural justice? Was Bligh's conduct sufficiently intolerable to excuse Christian's act of rebellion? It is the moral issues behind the dramatic incidents of the mutiny and the battle between opposing personalities that

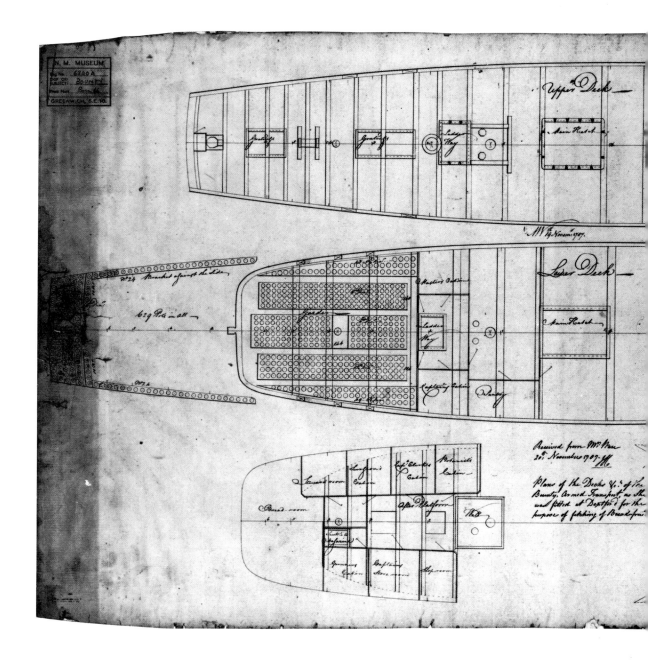

Deck Plan of HMS Bounty, *showing fittings for breadfruit transport, 20 November 1787. Kindly lent by the National Maritime Museum, London (No.18)*
Shows the detailed arrangements made in the refitting to accommodate the pots containing breadfruit plants. The space required reduction of the Commander's cabin space. The crowded conditions for officers and crew on the small ship were to prove disastrous.

makes the story so compelling, and has brought out competing protagonists for one side or the other from 1790 to the present day. The failure to round Cape Horn, the long sojourn in Tahiti, the slow breakdown of relationships, the small size of the ship, the absence of a second commissioned officer to support Bligh, the poor quality of the crew, all contributed to create an atmosphere favourable to mutiny. But the event, when it took place, appears to have been spontaneous and unpremeditated. Christian in the depths of despair was contemplating pushing off from the *Bounty* on a raft, so desperate was he to get away, when the midshipman Edward Young suggested that several of the crew were with him and would help him to take the ship instead. Like many great events with weighty consequences, the mutiny was a brief, casual and confused affair. Few people were clear what was happening, loyalties were divided, and the sequence of events leading to the dispatch of the launch was haphazard. Alone of the mutineers, Christian

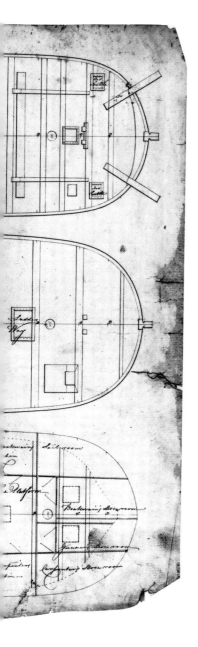

seems to have been aware of the enormity of the step he was taking, placing him beyond the bounds of society. The constant repetition of the refrain, "I am in hell", confirms that he was at breaking point and unable to help himself.

Bligh's 3,618 mile crossing of the Timor Sea in an open boat with 18 loyalists and a limited stock of food is rightly celebrated as one of the greatest feats of seamanship and navigation of all time. Bligh's confidence in himself, his unerring skills as a navigator, his continued control of his crew when in the last stages of exhaustion and destitution, demonstrate leadership of a high order. He was the right man for a crisis. The weather-stained log he kept in the launch is one of the chief treasures in the Exhibition. Seaman to the core, Bligh recorded the events of his voyage and surveyed the islands they passed as if he were carrying out normal duties aboard ship rather than struggling for survival.

M. Wilson and K. Britten. Model of HM Armed Transport Bounty, *1989. Kindly lent by the National Maritime Museum, London (No.15)*

This model was commissioned for the National Maritime Museum's 1989 Mutiny on the Bounty *Exhibition. It faithfully shows all details including the three ship's boats — a cutter, jolly boat and the famous launch or longboat intended for surveys in shallow waters.*

George Dashwood. *View in Pitcaine's [sic] Island, 1833.* SLNSW (No.63)

HMS Challenger *visited the Island in January 1833. Lieutenant Dashwood's sketch shows the slab huts lived in by descendants of the mutineers and the Tahitian women who went with them.*

The fate of the mutineers was no less dramatic than that of the loyalists. The seizure of those who remained in Tahiti by Captain Edwards of the *Pandora*, the shipwreck of that vessel off the Barrier Reef, and the adventures of the survivors, is a story in itself. The subsequent trial of the mutineers, and the execution of three of them, witnessed the start of the *Bounty* controversy. Bligh had returned to London in 1790 as the hero of the hour, the victim of a mutiny, who had survived an incredible ordeal against all the odds. By the time of the trial, he was aboard the *Providence*, completing the second and successful breadfruit voyage. Now was the time for the supporters of the mutineers to come forward, in particular Edward Christian, the barrister brother of Fletcher, and Nessy Heywood, who secured a pardon for brother Peter Heywood.

Edward Christian's *Appendix* to Stephen Barney's *Minutes of the Court-Martial*, based on interviews with the *Bounty* crew, and dressed up in legalistic form, was a clever piece of character assassination, building up a picture of a capricious and sadistic captain to explain, if not to excuse, his brother's conduct. From then on the battle was joined. Countless books and articles have been written and films produced to try and demonstrate what really happened on the *Bounty*, who was right and who was wrong, and what, in the final event, is the lesson to be learnt. The fate of the mutineers who escaped to Pitcairn is perhaps the strangest of all. The isolated settlement, beset by tensions between the whites and natives, became the scene for a sequence of murders the details of which remain unclear. From bloodshed was born a remarkable community, led by the sole white survivor, John Adams, who adjured alcohol and took to the Bible. The island was rediscovered in the early 19th century, and the evidence of the venerable patriarch helped to fill in a number of gaps in the *Bounty* story. The old mutineer himself was wisely left in peace.

The mutiny and its consequences dominate the foreground of the *Bounty* story. The wider context in which the voyage took place is often overlooked or misunderstood. Bligh had been commissioned to transport breadfruit plants from Tahiti to the West Indies as a new source of food supplies for the

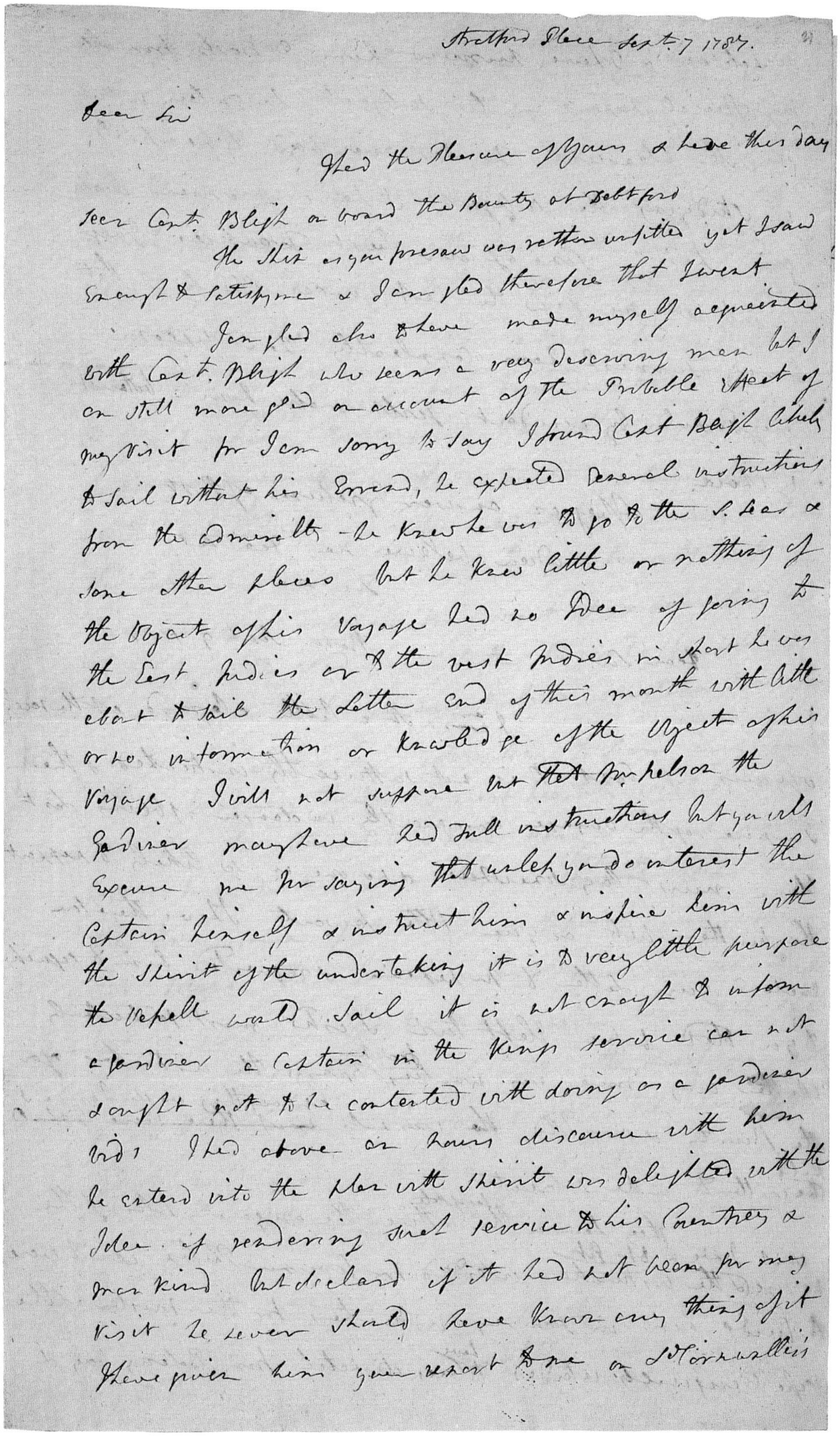

Stratford Place Sept. 7 1787.

Dear Sir

Agreeable to the Pleasure of yours I have this day seen Capt. Bligh on board the Bounty at Deptford

The Ship as you presume was rather unfitted yet I saw Enough to Satisfy me & I am glad therefore that I went

I am glad also to have made myself acquainted with Capt. Bligh who seems a very discerning man but I am still more glad on account of the Probable Effect of my visit for I am sorry to say I found Capt Bligh likely to sail without his Errand, he expected several instructions from the Admiralty – he knew he was to go to the S. Seas & some other places but he knew little or nothing of the Object of his Voyage had no Idea of going to the East Indies or to the West Indies in short he was about to sail the latter end of this month with little or no information or knowledge of the Object of his Voyage. I will not suppose but ~~that~~ Mr Nelson the Gardiner may have had full instructions but you will Excuse me for saying that unless you do interest the Captain himself & instruct him & inspire him with the Spirit of the undertaking it is to very little purpose the Vessell would sail it is not enough to inform a Gardiner a Captain in the Kings service can not & ought not to be contented with doing as a Gardiner

Indeed I had above six hours discourse with him he entered into the Plan with Spirit was delighted with the Idea of rendering such service to his Countrey & mankind but declared if it had not been for my visit he never should have known any thing of it

I have given him your report to me on M Marsalles's

'I am glad also to have made myself acquainted with Capt. Bligh who seems a very discerning man . . .' *In this letter of 7 September 1787 to Sir George Young, Sir Joseph Banks records his first impressions of William Bligh. Banks proved to be a powerful sponsor and life-long friend of Bligh.* SLNSW *(No. 16)*

HMS Bounty*'s Chronometer, made by Larcum Kendall, London, 1771. Kindly lent by the National Maritime Museum, London (No.20)*

This famous instrument is similar to the prototype devised by John Harrison which enabled accurate recording of longitude. It was issued to Bligh in 1787 and was retained by the mutineers on the Bounty*. In 1808 John Adams gave it to an American whaling captain, who in turn gave it to the Governor of Juan Fernandes. The chronometer was returned to London in 1843.*

William Hodges. War Canoe, Otaheite, 1774. SLNSW (No.2)

The first images of Tahiti seen by Europeans were those drawn by the artists on Captain Cook's Second Voyage, which visited the island in 1773 and 1774. William Hodges, a professional artist, was very successful in capturing the exotic scenery and ceremonies.

Matthew Flinders. A Sketch of the Island Wytootackee, 1792? SLNSW (No.122)

Flinders served under Bligh as a junior midshipman on HMS Providence. Some of the minor plans for the voyage were executed by him. His small monogram (MF) appears at the intersection of the true meridian and the parallel of latitude.

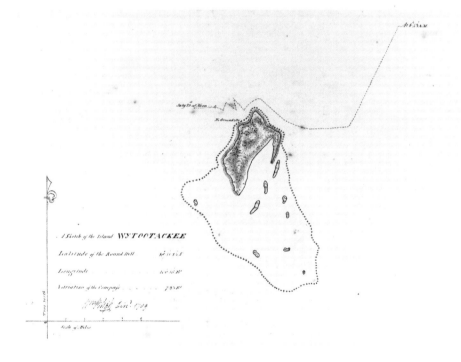

slaves there. The reasons for what may appear a rather bizarre enterprise require some explanation. In the first place, it is important to stress that the voyage of the *Bounty* was a naval expedition. You cannot understand the character of the voyage without understanding its specifically naval context. Whereas early voyages of discovery in the 16th and 17th centuries had often been privately financed, and undertaken in the expectation of profit, those of the 18th century had become the preserve of the Navy. No other body was capable of financing them, since they had no immediate commercial benefits. No other body possessed the specialized ships and equipment necessary to equip such voyages for long periods in unknown waters. No other body could provide the technological skills and know how.

Henry Roberts. Huaheine, one of the Society Islands, 1773? SLNSW (No.1)

The Navy had various reasons for promoting voyages of exploration. In the first place, there was the disinterested scientific reason of finding out more about uncharted regions of the globe. There was also the desire to aid commerce and colonization. New lands might be a source of wealth and power to those who discovered them first: beating the opposition played no small part in naval thinking. Finally there were the strategic advantages that flowed from improved knowledge of sea-routes, navigable channels and straits, coastlines and ports. The surveying work of these expeditions formed no small part of that achievement. They made for safer and faster means of communication, and gave inestimable advantages to the naval power that possessed them. By the end of the Seven Years War in 1763, the British Navy was pre-eminent in many parts of the world. Their warships, supplied by a succession of trading posts and colonial outstations, controlled the sealanes to the Indian Ocean and the Far East, across the Atlantic to the American colonies and the West Indies, and they constituted a formidable presence in the Mediterranean and the North Sea. The work of the naval explorers was an extension of the work of patrolling the seaways of the world, helping to defend British possessions and to extend her interests.

The most famous of the voyages were those undertaken by Captain James Cook. In little more than a decade his discoveries had totally transformed the state of European knowledge about the Pacific Region. It is no surprise to find that Bligh had served with Cook on his third and final voyage, and had inherited his mantle as a pre-eminent navigator. Matthew Flinders, having served under Bligh, went on to survey the Australian coastline, and in his turn, inspired Sir John Franklin, the most famous of the early 19th century Arctic explorers. As the secrets of the Pacific unfolded, the new challenge was the discovery of the North-west Passage. It would be naval explorers and naval ships that would solve the riddle. The power of the Navy in the second half of the 18th century was formidable. The task of keeping the world's largest fleet in operation required a huge and complex organization. The Royal Dockyards, for example, represented industrial production and maintenance output on a scale unparalleled elsewhere in Britain. Supplying the ships, recruiting and training the crews, and laying down the conditions

Artist unknown. Portrait of Nathaniel Portlock. Kindly lent by the National Maritime Museum, London (No. 117)
The American born Portlock had been Master's mate on Cook's Third Voyage and hence a colleague of the young William Bligh. He was chosen as commander of the tender HMS Assistant on the Second Breadfruit Voyage, and showed great skill in charting and seamanship.

of service, called for a wide administrative network. The navy prided itself on high professional standards, the calibre of its officers and seamen, and the quality of its leadership. Confidence in the effectiveness of the service was overwhelming.

That confidence had been shaken but not undermined by the experiences of the American War of Independence, 1778-82. Britain had entered a war for the first time without European allies, and faced a hostile combination of French, Spanish and Dutch navies that outnumbered her own. Defending her home shores, supplying the forces in North America, protecting trade and overseas possessions, proved too great a strain. The American colonies were lost, but in the closing stages of the war Britain countered the strategic threat in the Channel and the Caribbean, winning a series of engagements, most notably Rodney's victory at the Battle of the Saints in 1783. Britain had learned her lesson. The Navy went through a process of strengthening and reorganization which stood the nation in good stead when war broke out once more, in 1793 three years after the *Bounty* mutiny. It was the Navy which stood between revolutionary France and the subjugation of Europe, as Britain's European allies suffered successive defeats. It was naval successes which lit up a scene of prevailing gloom and defeat.

Captain Bligh was to play no small part in those heroic events of the Napoleonic period, and he ended his career with the rank of Vice-Admiral. The mutiny had been merely a temporary slip in the career of an otherwise exemplary naval officer. It must have left its scars, but it affected neither Bligh's bouncy self-confidence in himself nor his ambition. It was he who received the surrender of the Dutch flagship at the Battle of Camperdown in 1797, and he who was commended by Nelson for his gallantry at Copenhagen in 1801. He later became Governor of New South Wales, and the victim of a new form of mutiny. His attempts to tackle colonial abuses were thwarted by a combination of corrupt military officers and self-interested local politicians. Bligh was simply out of his depth, and few useful parallels can be drawn with the earlier *Bounty* mutiny.

Bligh was over-zealous, a martinet and disciplinarian, with a blinkered view of human nature that flawed him as a commander. Nevertheless, he was a seaman of high abilities and an outstanding navigator, against whom circumstances conspired in 1789 to bring out his worst faults and blind spots. The story of the mutiny continues to revolve around this powerful and unpredictable personality.

Richard Ormond is Director of the National Maritime Museum, Greenwich.

MUTINEER WHO MADE HISTORY

Glynn Christian

Fletcher Christian and William Bligh had more in common than friendship, mutual career patronage and family neighbourliness on the Isle of Man where they lived. They were both driven by a distinct and unshakeable expectation of their place in the future and a profound belief in their inherent right to rule other men. Christian's was based on birthright and confidence in the extraordinary pattern of his family's service to others through the administration of justice for more than three centuries. Bligh's was based on the authority and marble-like sense of righteousness he believed he donned with his naval uniform. They were classic, immovable objects, fuelled by the same irresistible force.

Bounty's muster shows Fletcher Christian to have been 21 when he signed on as master's mate, but this is not true. He was 22 and would be 23, weeks later, on 25 September 1787. In contrast to Bligh's startling porcelain-white skin, Fletcher Christian was brown-skinned and darkhaired. He was 5ft 10 inches, and his body was muscular; throughout his recorded life, other men told of his physical strength and his delight in it — he could make a standing jump from one barrel directly in to another and would hold a heavy musket at arm's length so that it might be measured how straight it was. His appearance was marred only by a slight outward bending of his knees, which the breeches of his midshipman's uniform would emphasize into the appearance of being positively bow-legged. Perhaps symptomatic of a nervous propensity, he was subject to violent sweats, particularly in the palms of his hands. Bligh, who was the only one to comment on this, said that unless he constantly carried handkerchiefs he would sully anything he touched.

For all his fame we do not know what Fletcher Christian looked like. There are images about, but these are as likely to be accurate as the features of Marlon Brando or David Essex who have portrayed him. The nearest we might get is the picture of Christian watching Bligh in the long boat in Dodd's famous oil painting and subsequent prints. Bligh approved the original after his epic return and is thought to have helped to correct the likeness of the men portrayed. There is a wicked contemporary irony in the picture, little understood these days, but as barbed as a modern *Private Eye* cartoon. Christian is standing precisely where in reality Bligh's private lavatory would have been cantilevered over the stern . . .

Fletcher Christian was born in 1764 at Moorland Close, tucked just below the brow of a hill which slopes eventually to Cockermouth on the edge of Cumbria's Lake District. He was christened the same day, named after his maternal grandmother's family, in Brigham church. His first school was here, too, in Eller Cottage which may still be seen. Next he went on, by piebald

Fletcher Christian. Detail from the painting by Robert Dodd. The Mutineers turning Lieut. Bligh and part of the Officers and Crew adrift from His Majesty's Ship The Bounty, 1790. SLNSW (No. 33)

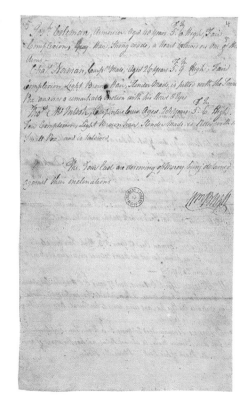

'Fletcher Christian, Masters Mate, Aged 24 Years 5 F.9In. High, Blackish or very dark brown Complexion, Dark Brown hair, Strong Made, a Star tatowed on his left breast, tatowed on the Backside, his knees Stands a little out, and he may be called rather Bow legged. He is Subject to Violent perspirations, and particularly in his hands so that he soils anything he handles.'

Manuscript of a description of the mutineers signed by William Bligh. The description was written at Batavia to assist in the recognition and arrest of the mutineers. At the end of the description Bligh makes a bid for clemency for four crew members detained aboard the Bounty against their will.

SLNSW (No. 30)

pony we are told, to the Cockermouth Free Grammar School. He was there at the same time as William Wordsworth, but stories of their friendship are silly. Christian was six years older and schoolboys rarely fraternize over such a wide age gap; even brothers do not. In fact, a brother, Edward Christian, later taught Wordsworth English and acted for William and his sister Dorothy, winning for them their celebrated case against Clive of India.

Fletcher then followed his brothers to St Bees School, close to Whitehaven, a venerable institution then and now founded by charter of Elizabeth I in 1583 and closely linked to Queen's College Oxford, which now owns Moorland Close. The Catechism, Latin, Greek, Mathematics and Navigation were the ingredients of a young gentleman's education and Fletcher was a good scholar. Brother Edward, when he was later defending him, pointed out that Fletcher Christian had stayed at school far longer than most young men who joined the Navy. This is true, but it is unlikely that the sea had any place in Fletcher's plans until the greed of his older brothers and his mother's financial disabilities cruelly and abruptly ended his education. Instead of continuing to Cambridge, following a centuries-old family tradition, he had nothing presently or for the future.

His mother Ann Christian, widowed when Fletcher was four, was bankrupted when he was 16, owing more than £6,000 (probably £¼ million today). Moorland Close and the income its land produced was no more. His father's family, the Christians of Milntown on the Isle of Man and Ewanrigg (above Maryport in Cumbria), had already done more than their share by previously bailing out Ann and her fatherless brood and by lending constantly to her older sons to finance their fine educations and law practices in London and Cockermouth. In future, Fletcher had only himself to rely upon.

Fletcher's direct Christian ancestors had been recorded in the Isle of Man since 1380, beyond which few records are reliable anyway. The long line of grandfathers had numerical suffixes, to ease the confusion caused by the constant use of Ewan, William and John as first names. We know much about them, for by unwritten hereditary right the Christians of Milntown, close to Ramsey in the north of the Isle of Man, were First Deemsters, judiciary heads responsible for the administration of the unwritten laws of the island. For generations they had acted as interpreters and buffers between the uncrowned kings of Man (such English aristocrats as the Earls of Derby) and the people of Man, and were specially respected for the trouble they took to be fair and to avoid the imposition of the death penalty. It was the family's defence of the island which made it the last area to capitulate to Cromwell, for which the Christians became the only family to suffer after the Restoration of Charles II in 1660 — not from the king of Great Britain, but from a piqued Earl of Derby who felt that his own kingship of Man could overrule the general pardon by the British king to all but regicides.

For more centuries than one can be sure, the Christians owned the best lands, made the best marriages, wielded almost unlimited power, and ruled by ancient right, might, and an army of bastards who, contrary to mainland practice, took the surname of their fathers. Political expediency in the wake of the Restoration saw them move their main seat to Cumberland and 42-bedroomed Ewanrigg. While keeping all their land and most of their influence, they were safe from the bloody thrust of politics and concentrated on filling coffers rather than coffins.

Now, late in the 18th century they were almost at their zenith. The sons being prepared to inherit, Fletcher's brothers and first cousins were destined to become memorable men in the corridors of Westminster and the Inns of

Court, in the Cabinet, the peerage, the Palaces of the Church, the government and commerce of India, the East and West Indies, the highest ranks of the Navy and universities and, most unforgettably, the newly discovered islands of the South Pacific. John XVII, the young head of the family, was as revolutionary and experimental as his ancestors, delivering England's first free milk, experimenting with winter animal feed, founding the first agricultural shows, and evolving for his mining employees friendly societies which were acknowledged in the 20th century as the pattern for the Welfare system.

Most families proudly point to men of power or wealth or influence in one generation or another; some even trace these attributes in several generations. But there are few, royalty and aristocracy included, who can claim the combination in an unbroken father-to-son line since the mid-14th century. The Christians could and it had a marked relevance to anyone born into the family. It would have been impossible for Fletcher Christian not to be influenced by the heritage and the expectation. In Georgian society he could now only beg, marry an heiress, or join the Navy. That he did the latter and was later often called ambitious meant something quite different in the 1780s than it does two centuries later. Ambition, the changing of the position into which you are born, was rare and thus it was commented on: you generally did more or less well in a position over which you had little control and less choice. The one acceptable way to change your social status was success in the Navy. Unlike the army, into or out of which you bought your way, the Navy promoted on ability — indeed you could be dismissed if you were found unfit for the responsibility of command in what was then Britain's most important and expensive means of defence. It was perfectly acceptable for men of common trade or agricultural background to be raised high in the Navy, and such success would give Christian back the status and role he was born to expect, and some income to go with it. Bligh had never wanted for income, but he too looked to the Navy for status and respect.

Frustrated love and marriage plans are likely further to have strengthened Fletcher's resolve. Considering that he later called his Tahitian wife Isabella, and that his name has many times been linked romantically with his relative, Isabella Curwen, it is perhaps poignant that in April 1783, six months after Isabella married his cousin John XVII (to whom she was even more closely related), he signed on as a midshipman aboard HMS *Eurydice*; there is no evidence to support the claim that in 1782/3 he served aboard HMS *Cambridge* when Bligh was this ship's sixth lieutenant — he was a boarder at St Bees, in the Isle of Man with his mother and sister, or both. Isabella Curwen was prodigiously rich and beautiful and the sole heiress to one of the country's 10 oldest family names, a mining, shipping and agricultural fortune which neatly dovetailed into that of the Christians, and heiress to Workington Hall. Her trustees jumped to most of her whims, including the purchase of an amusing round house in an island in Lake Windermere; it was renamed Belle Isle for her and is still in the family. John XVII had regularly returned from his Grand Tour to court her and finally they eloped to Scotland. Marriage to Isabella Curwen would have been a sensible dynastic and financial step for Fletcher to have taken. But Isabella and he were both the same age. His older and incredibly richer cousin married her instead.

HMS *Eurydice*, Captain George Courtney, was a 6th rater, the last British naval ship able to be manoeuvred by oars. In October she sailed for India via the Cape of Good Hope, and in Madras Christian's naval career took a signal step upwards. Courtney made him an acting lieutenant and gave him charge of a watch during the return voyage. Fletcher was described on the voyage as strict, but someone who "ruled in a superior pleasant manner". To his brother Edward he said of his experiences on returning in June 1785: "It was very easy to make oneself beloved and respected aboard a ship; one had only to be always ready to obey one's superior officers, and to be kind to the common men, unless there was occasion for severity, and if you are when there is just occasion they will not like you the less for it."

Fletcher now decided he had enough experience to look for a better paid job in the merchant navy and sought a mate's posting on a West Indiaman. He was using family and friends' influence well enough to be treating with a merchant in the City when a relative arrived in London from the Isle of Man. Captain Taubman, who had been married to Fletcher's first cousin Dorothy Christian, said he would write to William Bligh, who had married the daughter of the Collector of Customs in the island, and who owed him some favours. Christian would certainly have met Bligh or his wife in Douglas, or at least knew of him, for his mother was often at the Nunnery, Taubman's mansion, and could hardly have avoided knowing Betsy Bligh in the small town. Bligh politely told Christian by letter that he had a full complement on the ship on which he was trading in the West Indies. Edward says that by return Fletcher wrote that "wages were no object, he only wished to learn his profession and if Captain Bligh would permit him to mess with the gentlemen he would readily enter the ship as a foremast man until there was a vacancy amongst the officers . . . We midshipmen are gentlemen. We never pull at a rope; I should even be glad to go one voyage in that situation for there may be occasions when officers are called upon to do the duties of a common man." Bligh agreed, but it was to be 15 months before they traded in the West Indies aboard *Britannia*. It was a mutually good arrangement in contemporary terms. Christian was learning from a man respected for his navigational skills; Bligh had done a favour for a member of the Christian clan and that was no bad thing. I think there was another reason for the strength of friendship and dependence which immediately sprang up between the two men. Although only 10 years older than Christian, Bligh seems to have been seen as the father Christian lost when he was four. Christian was the son Bligh did not, and would never, have.

It is not easy to discover exact details of the two men's trips aboard *Britannia*, except that when they returned to Britain at the end of the second one in August 1787 Bligh learned he was to lead an expedition to the South Seas. On their first voyage Christian had sailed as an ordinary seaman, but dined with the officers and middies (midshipmen). He told his family that Bligh had furthered his knowledge of navigation and that although a very passionate man he prided himself on knowing how to humour him. Of their second voyage, Edward Lamb, who is the only man ever to have criticized Christian for not doing his duty, wrote that Bligh was "blind to (Christian's) faults and had him to dine and sup every other day in the cabin, and treated him like a brother in giving him every information". Lamb also described Christian as "then one of the most foolish young men I ever knew in regard to (women)". His shipmate Lebogue who also sailed aboard *Bounty* is the one who later remembered Fletcher always having a girl with him in Tahiti.

Only one thing is certain about *Britannia*'s voyages. Bligh and Christian were firm friends, teacher and pupil, and pleased enough with one another for Bligh to recommend and request the appointment of Christian to *Bounty*. When the ship returned, Christian was certain to become a lieutenant years before Bligh had reached the same rank. Christian had thus been sought out for special responsibility and attention aboard *Eurydice* and *Britannia* and was

William Hodges. Owharee Harbour Huaheine, 1773. Kindly lent by the National Maritime Museum, London

well on the way to a laudable recovery from the family misfortunes. There was just one more sensational experience to add to the makeup of the young man who was about to sail from Britain forever.

The twin problems of bad weather and a dilatory Admiralty which so delayed the departure of *Bounty* proved a boon and a turning point for Fletcher Christian. It gave him an unexpected chance to meet his brother Charles, surgeon aboard the East Indiaman *Middlesex* (Captain Rogers), which was returning from India. Fletcher was so anxious to see his brother that he took a small boat out to meet *Middlesex* before she had anchored and the two men spent the evening together. Charles' unpublished biography is part of the Christian Family Archive recently placed on permanent loan at the Douglas Library and Museum. Charles remembers Fletcher's great physical strength and says he was "full of professional Ambition and Hope. He said: 'I delight to set the Men an Example. I not only can do every part of a common Sailor's Duty, but am on a par with a principal part of the Officers' "

Fletcher brought his brother up to date with family news — their sister was dead, and so was Uncle Edmund Law, Bishop of Carlisle. For his part, Charles had something to tell which few others knew and thus could not consider when dissecting the mutiny which was to follow. Incredible as it may seem, there had been a mutiny aboard *Middlesex* and Charles was one of the officers involved. He was not in chains, for mutiny in the East India Company was not a crime against the King. But the last conversations Fletcher had in England were about the proper duty of officers to their men, and the actions that could be taken against captains who were cruel or thoughtless, as Rogers had been. (Subsequently, Rogers was punished as heavily as the officers who mutinied against him).

Bounty's voyage to the South Seas stretched everyone to the limit. Christian was sent as emissary to the Marques de Brancheforte, Spanish Governor of Tenerife, representing Bligh. Once *Bounty* sailed from here, Bligh announced officially their destination for the first time and finalized the introduction of his revolutionary plans for the health of his crew, with new styles of diet, compulsory daily dancing, and, most humanely, the introduction of a three watch system which gave men four hours on and eight hours off. The new watch needed an officer in charge and once again Fletcher Christian found himself promoted to acting lieutenant, a hat trick of promotion and preference aboard three ships. This time he was second in command. It is often written that this was unfair to Fryer, an insult in fact. But Fryer knew, as modern men do not, that masters were never promoted at sea, and there were other reasons for the tensions between him and Bligh. Indeed, Christian was probably promoted as a buffer between the two.

The story of *Bounty*'s failure to round Cape Horn and subsequent uncomfortable trek to Cape Town, dogged by discomfort as the wind direction meant the galley fires belched smoke throughout the living quarters, is more remarkable to me for the fact that Bligh had not lost a single man through ill health, whereas other ships arriving directly from Europe came with stories of scurvy and death.

There has long been a persistent thread of gossip that Cape Town was where Bligh and Christian first fell out. Adams, the sole male survivor of the settlement of Pitcairn, said that he believed Christian to be under some obligation to Bligh and that their original quarrel happened there and was kept up until the time of the mutiny. Certainly Christian was under obligation to Bligh for his posting to *Bounty* and for his promotion, but Bligh gives flesh to the bones of another rumour which later came from Christian's descendants, that of financial dependence. In his own correspondence in the Mitchell Library, Australia, Bligh writes to Edward Christian, reminding him that Fletcher had money whenever he wanted. Nothing comes between friends as easily as money and Bligh's famous ability to wound with words rather than action would have enjoyed nagging at something like this. The voyage eastwards to Tahiti was unremarkable for Christian. Midshipman Peter Heywood, another with Manx connections, said that Christian spent time helping him complete his education, with lessons in mathematics and classical languages.

In Tahiti, Christian's position aboard *Bounty* was strong enough to earn him the plum job, as commander of the shore party first collecting then guarding the breadfruit plants which were the object of the voyage. The spread of varieties of breadfruit tree means that one at least is in season all year round, and as they do not reproduce by seed but by suckers and shoots *Bounty*'s gardener Nelson was able to organize collection parties on 7 November 1788, and by the 15th they had 774, almost all they needed. Within a fortnight of arriving, the task was all but completed, and allowing for repairs and some certainty that the young shoots were healthy and growing, *Bounty* could have set sail in a month or so. Instead she stayed 20 weeks: *Bounty* was the first British ship to spend the summer's rainy season in Tahiti. The season still brings hurricanes and even today small ships prefer not to be exposed in the Pacific. It was too dangerous for Bligh to follow his orders and set sail, for even if he crossed the Pacific safely westward the prevailing winds at that time would have prevented him from entering the Endeavour Straits, north of Australia. For Christian, it was another unexpected watershed.

William Hodges. View of the Island of Otaha and Bola Bola with part of the Island of Ulietea, 1773-1774. Kindly lent by the National Maritime Museum, London (No.9)

These oil paintings were commissioned by the Admiralty on the return of Cook's Second Voyage and for many years hung at Admiralty House, Whitehall. Hodges painted them from his sketches and watercolours done on the Voyage and they evoke the lush landscape of the South Pacific islands.

John Webber. A Dance in Otaheite, c.1781-3. SLNSW (No.25)

While *Bounty* swayed in the pleasant breezes of Matavai Bay, Tahiti, and most of her men sweated and pined for life ashore, Christian had little to do but enjoy life in the breadfruit camp. He learned some Tahitian and went through the considerable pain and danger of tattooing. Most of all he was close to living the life he might have expected — as the benevolent master of land, its produce, and people. He may have been foolish about women, but that was acceptable here, provided you kept within the very detailed rules, stuck to your own equivalent class, and were prepared to accept some of the less savoury views of sex and its inevitable results — children. In Tahiti, a great proportion of female children was smothered at birth, as were children born to couples of mixed class, or who were members of the arioi secret society. Bligh had to deal with problems of deserters in Tahiti, but there is nothing to indicate tension between Bligh and Christian. That was to happen at sea, for in Tahiti, Fletcher Christian had finally grown into a man, independent, sexually experienced, and with a heightened sense of position and capability. He now wanted and expected something different from life; Bligh wanted exactly what he had enjoyed before. The suggestion that they were homosexual lovers is yet another theory based on the shifting sands of fashion and opportunistic publishing sensationalism. If there had been the slightest suspicion or evidence of this, the *Bounty* mutineers could tellingly have used it against Bligh at their trial. The penalty was death and Bligh, above all people, was too great a respecter of the law to break it in the pursuit of pleasure. He did not, remember, share the temptations of Tahiti, but remained faithful to his wife Betsy and his family.

Although Bligh publicly wrote that he and Christian never fell out over anything until immediately before the mutiny, his private papers tell a different story, corroborated by others aboard *Bounty*. Fryer says that after leaving Tahiti they "had some words when Mr Christian told Mr Bligh — 'Sir your abuse is so bad I cannot do my duty with any pleasure. I have been in hell for weeks with you'; several other disagreeable words passed which had been frequently the case."

The most public of these happened ashore at Nomuka, in the Friendly Islands. Christian was in charge of an armed watering party that was threatened by armed Polynesians — the first time this had happened. When

John Webber. Poedua, daughter of the chieftain of Raiatea, c.1785. Kindly lent by the National Library of Australia, Canberra (No.23)

Poedua was a young Tahitian princess held captive for 4 days on HMS Discovery *during Cook's Third Voyage. The beauty and charm of Tahitian girls were praised by the European visitors, and were a strong influence on the decision of the mutineers to return to Tahiti.*

Christian told Bligh that his party were unable to do their duty because of this, Bligh is said to have damned him for a cowardly rascal, asking if he were afraid of a "set of Naked Savages while he had Arms?" Christian replied: "The Arms are of no use while your orders prevent them from being used."

The later loss of a grapnel anchor angered Bligh so much that he kidnapped some of the islanders and sailed with them aboard, creating awful scenes of blood-letting and anguish in the small boats which followed until his prisoners were released.

It was irrational overreaction which amazed *Bounty*'s men, and for those in the firing line worse was to come. The "coconut incident" is astonishing for many reasons, but mostly because Bligh's published accounts do not mention it, whereas everyone else gives it great importance. In essence, Bligh publicly accused Fletcher Christian of theft: "Damn your blood you have stolen my coconuts." Christian replied that as he was dry, he thought it of no consequence to have taken one while on watch. "You lie, you scoundrel, you have stolen one half." Christian demanded to know why he was being

Richard Beechey. View of Watering Place at Gambier's Islands, 1826. SLNSW (No.62)

The Gambier or Manga Reva Islands lie north-west of Pitcairn Island, a short distance from Tahiti. The artist, Richard Beechey, was a midshipman on HMS Blossom, the first English vessel to make an official report on the fate of the mutineers.

treated like this; he had free access to Bligh's spirit supply simply by asking for the key — why should he bother to steal coconuts which had been bought at 20 for an iron nail! Bligh would not answer, clearly enjoying the hurt he was inflicting. And what hurt it was. Bligh was famous for his invective, knowing it was far more painful than sticks and stones. To accuse a gentleman, and his second in command, of so paltry a theft, and one which may have been imagined, was well beyond the boundaries of disciplinary requirements. No wonder Fletcher's brother Charles wrote: "What scurrilous abuse! What provoking insult . . . base, mean-minded wretch . . ."

It was more than that; it was breaking point.

Later that day Purcell the carpenter learned that there had been more abuse. Christian had run forward with tears welling and when asked what happened said: "Can you ask me and hear the treatment I receive?" When Purcell said that they all felt the same way, Christian reminded him that as a warrant officer he could not be flogged; "but if I should speak to him as you do he would probably break me, turn me before the mast, and perhaps flog me, and if he did it would be the death of us both, for I am sure I should take him in my arms and jump overboard with him." Even though an acting lieutenant, Christian was in fact still master's mate, a superior sort of midshipman, and could have been flogged as he said. Bligh's famous bullying knew how to stretch a man, but only to a point where he was thought not in danger of any back lash.

"I would rather die ten thousand deaths than bear this treatment. I always do my duty as an officer and a man ought to do, yet I receive this scandalous usage. Flesh and blood cannot bear this treatment," Christian wept. It was the first time men on board had seen him crying. "He was no milksop;" said one. Bligh knew that Christian's background made it unlikely that he would descend to battle with a superior officer or entertain any dereliction of duty. Instead, Christian decided that the only gentlemanly thing to do was to leave the ship, not a cowardly act, but by contemporary terms an honourable one. Late in the afternoon, Christian gave away his Polynesian curios, tore up his letters and papers, and threw them overboard. If he had planned to mutiny well in advance, there was no need to do this. Helping an officer desert his duty was a serious offence, but such was the sympathy aboard *Bounty* that Christian was collecting nails and other barter items from Purcell; with wood and bindings he was going to construct a raft and slip overboard to a new life.

In modern terms Christian may simply have been "doing something" to attract attention and to dissipate his frustrations. Christian was certainly a good enough navigator, linguist, and farmer to survive, and a single man was likely easily to have been assimilated. It is important to remember also that among the men who were aboard *Bounty*, Bligh was the only one who ever suggested that it was Tahiti or women which had inflamed Christian. Christian lashed two masts to his raft and hid some pork and breadfruit. His preparations were well observed, but he used the flimsy excuse to stay on board that there were too many men on deck at night to leave in secrecy.

What happened next has been the subject of much argument, and this is not the place to rehearse even one of the theories. Suffice to say that at some time during the night, when he slept for only one hour, or in the early minutes of his watch which began at 4am, Christian decided that it was not he who should leave the ship but Bligh. There was no well-conceived plan to take the ship, but simply a desire to rid the ship of Bligh and the worst of his gang. But *Bounty* was no ordinary ship. Her complement was the first all-volunteer crew to sail a naval vessel. They were free men who had chosen adventure and in return had tasted the pleasures of Tahiti and the South Pacific. Whatever had driven Fletcher to mutiny was not what suddenly ignited others to join him. The reported raging and pleading of Bligh with Christian — "you have dannled my children on your knees" — exposed for all to see the depth of their previous friendship and Christian's despair. His wild eyes and temperament have been used to suggest, among many theories, that he was suffering from syphilis; I expect most of us in the throes of leading a mutiny after one hour's sleep and weeks of torment would look something less than composed and in good health.

The largely unpublished life of Fletcher Christian after the mutiny gives the clearest views of his aspirations and beliefs. He may not have planned to mutiny, but like all those second in command he clearly had thought about what he might do as commander. He now embarked on a series of radical changes aboard *Bounty* which made him a true revolutionary. Months before the storming of the Bastille in Paris in the interests of liberty, equality, and fraternity, something of which he would have had no inkling, Fletcher Christian introduced democratic decision making aboard the ship. Leaders were elected, often from among those who had resisted Christian's actions; but men at sea are more sensible of their safety than to give authority only to those they liked. Far more telling than democracy was Christian's decision that everyone on board should have a uniform. In the 18th century, only the officers and gentlemen wore uniforms, but Christian believed that uniformity of dress created a sense of fraternity and would also present a more powerful image to others as he searched now for a safe haven. Thus jackets were stitched from sail cloth and edged with the blue of his own uniform. When later confronted by belligerent Polynesians, the uniforms appeared to have the desired effect, but the unity was barely skin deep. *Bounty* remained a ship of

Top
Norfolk, late Pitcairn Islanders, c.1860-1862. SLNSW (No.75)

From a photograph of some Pitcairn Islanders shortly after their resettlement, taken by a crew member of the visiting ship, HMS Pelorus

Above
Children of the Bounty, *Pitcairn Island, 20 July 1906. SLNSW (No.73)*

From a photograph taken by a crew member of HMS Cambrian *of the children of the original Pitcairn Islanders, who returned after a few unhappy years on Norfolk Island.*

Above right
George Tobin. Figures, called Ettee, Island of Otahytey, 1792, SLNSW (No.118)

suspicion, sailed by Christian's supporters and those who would have gone with Bligh.

After returning to Tahiti to collect livestock, and gathering also Tahitian men and women, Christian attempted to settle on Tubuai. It is a credit to his administrative ability that this motley and partly unwilling group was persuaded in the sickly subtropical heat to build a huge fortress of earth surrounded by a deep moat. But a political error meant the siting of the loyally-named Fort George had upset the mightiest chief in the island. War followed and Christian sailed his unhappy charges back to Tahiti. The future was put to the vote once more; Christian wanted only *Bounty* but found himself with eight followers as well. The rest, mutineers and Bligh loyalists alike, chose to stay in Tahiti.

In a decision which remains one of his most puzzling, Christian cut the anchor cable without warning early in the morning of 23 September 1789 and *Bounty* slipped through the reef. By daylight there had been a sort out and the ship headed back to Moorea, releasing six "rather ancient" women who had been among those trapped, but who had not found the companion or other reason to stay. On board was Mauatua who was to bear Christian's three children, but there is no evidence that they had previously been lovers, and he was never said to have had a single attachment. She may have been older than he for she remembered the visits of Captain Cook and many years later said that she had left children in Tahiti. Also aboard was a baby girl, who was eventually to marry Charles, the second son she bore to Fletcher; all his grandchildren were more Tahitian than English. Christian called his companion Isabella and others called her Mainmast for her upright bearing; this later became Maimiti in the Pitcairn dialogue and this is the name generally used in film and stage depictions.

It was only in the 1950s that Professor Maude of Canberra finally pieced together the long trek *Bounty* now made with eight European men, six Tahitian men, and 14 females, including the baby. Far from the usual indication that she sailed southwards to Pitcairn, *Bounty* sailed west as far as the Fijian islands. On the way she discovered Rarotonga, and probably introduced the orange, now a mainstay of that economy. In the Fijians, it became finally clear that populated islands would never offer safety. Christian's constant studying of the charts left in Bligh's cabin focused on Pitcairn's Island. Remote, uninhabited, and difficult to land at — it was perfect, but it was almost 2,000 miles and a month's sailing back the way they had come. To me, the fact that *Bounty*, seriously undermanned by a group of men and women who spoke little of each other's language and knew less of each other's culture, could now choose to sail with Christian deep in to the colder southern waters of the Pacific is wonderful. That there was eventually some discussion about returning to Tahiti if Pitcairn had not been found seems perfectly reasonable; to suggest that Fletcher had no qualities of leadership is puerile. The voyage took two chill and dispiriting months.

When *Bounty* finally reached the position Pitcairn was supposed to occupy there was only sea. It had been charted incorrectly and Christian now knew his decision was right. If he could find Pitcairn no one in the world was likely to guess where they were or to find them. He zig zagged carefully, using all navigational skills and eventually found it on the evening of 15 January 1790. Only a mile by a mile by a mile and a half, it is remoteness itself, and the community was not discovered until 1808. The new society founded as a result of Christian's single, precipitate decision had no help from precedent. The Tahitians had to break down further the taboos that shipboard life prevented anyway — back home women were not allowed to touch much of the food men ate, for instance. The Europeans saw themselves as landed gentry and quickly turned the Tahitian men into servants and slaves, aping positions in society they could never have aspired to at home. The end was inevitable. More mutiny, this time by black men against white. In October 1793, on the day his third child Mary was born, Christian was shot and clubbed as he worked in his garden. There he undoubtedly died. The two-century-old industry in *Bounty*/Bligh/Christian surmize has largely been fanned by the possibility that Christian escaped Pitcairn and returned to Britain. It is indeed possible. But assiduous checking of each of the 11 conflicting stories of his death, including visiting Pitcairn Island itself, proved to me that none had credibility.

As with so many heroes of protest and escapism, it seems that the public did not and does not want Christian to have died ignominiously with his broken head blackening in the red soil of Pitcairn; Christian was given the 18th and 19th century treatment that tabloids give to Elvis Presley and James Dean today, though abetted by the dissembling of Adams and the misunderstanding of early visitors who were dissuaded from speaking to the surviving Tahitian women. To those who understand such things, Fletcher Christian is one of the finest navigators of his time, a shining pupil of Bligh, who in return reflected the brilliance of Cook. With the help of Larcum's newly perfected chronometer, Christian was safely to sail the undermanned ship 8,000 miles in search of a home and founded a brave new world of his own.

Richard Beechey. Landing at Bounty Bay, *c.1825. SLNSW (No.64)*

The rough surf of Bounty Bay made landing on Pitcairn Island difficult. Here crewmen from HMS Blossom *steer for the narrow shore between the rocks on the crest of a breaker, with two men on shore as watchers.*

Christian was a law-breaker, a mutineer, a pirate, a blackbirder, and probably a fool. He was also an important, but unheralded explorer, the founding father of a unique people, and like so many of his powerful family a courageous social pioneer. What Rousseau dreamed, Christian did. His descendants became the most God-fearing community on earth and thus it is through the Victorian Church, which adapted the *Bounty* story as a modern parable, that the 19th century was fed a constant flow of Pitcairn and *Bounty* fable. But there was no myth about the legacy of fairness and justice that Fletcher left his island, for Pitcairn was the first community in the world to give women a full franchise.

There never was a mutiny of the *Bounty*. Rather was there a revolt by one man against another, Christian against Bligh. Logically, that clash can only be understood if the passions and perversities of both men are understood. In the bibliography of more than 2,500 books and articles there remains only one biography of Fletcher Christian, proof indeed that this is a story which touches some seminal core: the truth about Fletcher Christian is less important to many people than what he has come to represent, or how he can be manipulated to enhance the reputation of other heroes. When I first began to research my ancestor, I expected to whiten Bligh and blacken Christian, but the contemporary facts do not allow this. Now I look forward to the day when there is no longer the urge to cast Bligh or Christian as black or white, but simply to remember them as they were. Blame does not matter today. They are men who are remembered. Few men who are remembered for as long and as thrillingly as they, can have been wholly black or white.

Glynn Christian is the only biographer, and a direct descendent, of Fletcher Christian and well-known in the United Kingdom as a television chef and cookery writer.

TRAGEDY OF THE *PANDORA*

Ronald A. Coleman

The story of the mutiny and Bligh's epic open boat voyage of 3,618 nautical miles created an immediate sensation in England. Bligh was a hero. The mutineers, whose side of the story would not be known for two and a half more years, were the lowest of scoundrels and common pirates.

Bligh had arrived in England from the Cape of Good Hope on 14 March 1790. Within nine days of his arrival, his friend and influential patron, Sir Joseph Banks, had obtained the King's permission for him to publish his narrative of *Bounty*'s voyage. By Royal Navy custom, Bligh would have to face a court-martial to answer for the loss of his ship. But this would not take place for some months as the remainder of his surviving *Bounty* crew had not yet arrived from the Cape and they would be required to attend as well. The protracted delay would cause Bligh some anxiety. However, it would also give him time to consolidate his version of the voyage without fear of contradiction from the troublemakers Fryer and Purcell.

Unbeknown to Bligh and Banks, Secretary of State William Grenville was, at that very time, drafting orders for a secret mission to the Pacific of great importance. It was to have considerable bearing on government's eventual plan to pursue and apprehend the *Bounty* mutineers.

To the Admiralty, mutiny was a most serious breach of Royal Navy discipline. The mutineers could not be left unpunished. In many ways, the necessity to do something about the *Bounty* was a complication which might endanger Grenville's scheme. He did not want attention focused on the Pacific for the moment. On the other hand, perhaps the *Bounty* problem could be used to his advantage.

Two months before Bligh's return, the government had received news that two private English fur-trading vessels had been seized by Spanish warships at Nootka Sound on the north-western coast of America. The seizure was not overly alarming, but would require a routine demand through diplomatic channels that the ships be released. However, the second part of the news was electrifying. The Spanish ships were establishing a permanent settlement at Nootka.

For two centuries, attempts had been made to discover a North-west Passage between the Atlantic and the Pacific. Since Canada had become an English colony after the Seven Years War, that the passage, if it existed, be English controlled was imperative. At virtually the same time as news of the Nootka incident was received, information was also received from Quebec which had implications of supreme importance. Fur-trapper and explorer Peter Pond had discovered what he believed to be two major rivers flowing from Great Slave Lake in central Canada towards the Pacific. The first flowed

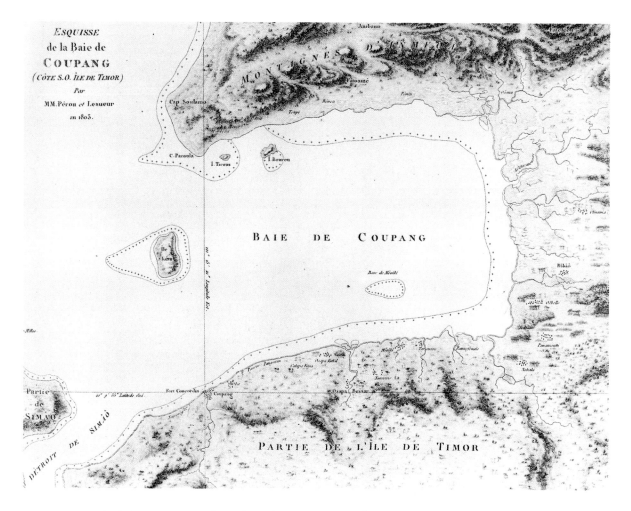

After the mutiny on 28 April 1789, Bligh and 18 loyal crew members were cast adrift in the Bounty's *launch, a 23 foot (7m.) longboat. In a consummate feat of navigation without instruments, Bligh guided the boat 3,618 nautical miles in 41 days, reaching Kupang Harbour on 14 July 1789*

westwards and might empty into the sea near Cook's Inlet or Prince William Sound at the base of the Alaskan peninsula. The second flowed southwards through a chain of other lakes and possibly met the sea near Queen Charlotte's Sound, only 100 nautical miles north of Nootka. The southern alternative was the more desirable as it would be ice-free for longer periods of the year. If it turned out to be the passage, the Spaniards were getting too close.

Spain had traditionally clung to her ancient pretension to sovereignty over the American continents and all the seas west of a line, drawn by the Treaty of Tordesillas in 1494, which divided the world between her and Portugal. Discovery and acts of proclamation were, as far as she was concerned, sufficient to secure possession of new territories. England contended that permanent settlement and active development were necessary to achieve sovereignty over a newly discovered land. This difference of opinion had caused rifts between the two countries on several occasions in the past. However, now it appeared that Spain was playing the game by England's rules and England, therefore, had no grounds for protest about Spain's claim to Nootka. But Nootka Sound was on an island (Vancouver Island) and not the mainland. If England could immediately establish a settlement on the mainland at Queen Charlotte's Sound, she could then legitimately claim possession of the coast for a considerable distance to the north and south encompassing what may be the entrance to the illusive North-west Passage. It must be done in the utmost secrecy for if the Spanish were to get wind of

Grenville's intentions, they were in a position to beat England to it.

In view of this, the immediate despatch of a warship in pursuit of the *Bounty* mutineers might be suspected by the Spanish as a pretext to pose a naval threat at Nootka and put them on their guard. Two vessels of the secret squadron, *Gorgon* and *Discovery*, were expected to sail from England within weeks and Grenville needed a distraction. Also, there was the problem that the government needed to be seen doing something about *Bounty*.

In late March, the following article appeared in the *London Register*:

> It is said that by the express command of His Majesty two new sloops of war, one of them the *Hound* now on the stocks at Deptford, are to be instantly fitted to go in pursuit of the pirates who have taken possession of the *Bounty*. An experienced officer will be appointed to superintend the little command, and the sloops will steer a direct course to Otaheite (Tahiti) where, it is conjectured, the mutinous crew have established their rendezvous.

The article would serve two useful purposes. It would let the English public and the Spanish know that something was being done about *Bounty*, but *Hound* being still on the stocks, could not sail before the northern summer. By then, the secret fleet would be well on its way and it was *Gorgon*'s orders which included the real plan to search for the mutineers.

Parts of Grenville's scheme had been put into effect when in the following month new information was received. Not two, but four vessels had been seized. And, most importantly, English fur-traders had established a permanent settlement at Nootka in the name of King George *before* the Spanish ships had arrived. On the face of it, the Spanish commander had invaded English sovereign territory. The Prime Minister William Pitt's government now had the excuse they needed to threaten Spain with war. England would first demand the immediate restoration of the settlement at Nootka. She would then force a resolution of the differing doctrines of colonial sovereignty on the basis that Spain had disavowed England's rightful claim of sovereignty over Nootka. This would open up all unsettled territories in the Americas and give England freedom of all the seas traditionally claimed by Spain under the Tordesillas Treaty. Grenville's secret plan was shelved and in the first week of May the King announced to Parliament Cabinet's decision to mobilize the English fleet.

One ship to be brought out of mothballs for the purpose was HMS *Pandora*, a sixth-rate frigate of 24 guns.

The ship, with her masts and bowsprit, cannon and sea-going stores removed, had ridden at her moorings at Chatham since September 1783. She had been launched in May 1779 from the Deptford shipyard of Henry Adams and William Barnard to meet the needs of the American War. *Pandora* had initially served in the Channel Fleet during the unsuccessful French and Spanish invasion of England in 1779, then as a convoy escort between England and Quebec, and lastly, as a lone cruiser off the American east coast credited with taking at least nine rebel ships as prizes under the command of Captain John Inglis.

An Admiralty warrant now ordered Chatham Dockyard to refit *Pandora* for another tour of duty in the Channel Fleet. On 6 August, Captain Edward Edwards received his commission to take command of the ship. His appointment from half-pay to *Pandora* had been the result of a recommendation by Lord Ducie under whom he had served as first lieutenant on *Augusta* (64) in the early stages of the American War. Edwards arrived at Chatham, read his orders to the crew, and hoisted his pennant on 10 August. However, the ship's original orders were not to be long lived. The

following day he received a letter from the Secretary of the Admiralty "directing me to attend Lord Chatham (the First Lord and brother of the Prime Minister) at the Admiralty without loss of time & informing me that a week's leave of absence was directed to be given me for that purpose."

On his return to the dockyard at Chatham on 17 August, he recorded in the ship's log that he had been "directed to fit the ship for a South Sea Voyage". Bearing in mind that the government, which, we have seen, had a penchant for finesse, was urgently preparing ships to be despatched to every corner of the globe in readiness to attack Spain and her possessions, is it mere coincidence that *Pandora* was now the only warship being sent to the Pacific where the cause of the conflict was centred? Possibly. The *Bounty* problem was still outstanding. The secret north-west coast expedition which had included a plan to capture the mutineers had been abandoned, and the story of the *Hound* and the other sloop had been nothing more than a red herring. Still, it is tempting to speculate on what other Pacific Ocean matters Lord Chatham may have discussed during Edwards' visit.

In September, another most curious article appeared in a publication with the impressive title, *The Lady's Magazine or Entertaining Companion for the Fair Sex, Appropriated solely to their Use and Amusement*. It was a magazine much read by wives of influential men and it said:

> The *Pandora* frigate is preparing at Chatham for a voyage to the South Seas; the object which the *Bounty* sailed from England to effect has been consigned to this ship: two botanists are to embark in her for the preservation of the breadfruit trees.

The prospect of a second breadfruit voyage had been a subject of discussion since Bligh's return. No documentary evidence has yet been found to show that *Pandora* was ever intended for this purpose. However, certain things do suggest that this may have been considered at some stage of the voyage's planning.

Once the ship's equipment was completed, which included the removal of several internal bulkheads to make room for 12 months' stores and victuals for *Pandora*'s own use as well as a complete set of stores to refit and provision the *Bounty*, there was little room for anything else. The ship's surgeon, George Hamilton, was later to write:

> What rendered our situation still more distressing was the crowded state of the ship, being filled to the hatchways with stores and provisions, for, like weevils, we had to eat a hole in our bread before we had a place to lay down in; every officer's cabin, the Captain's not excepted, being filled with provisions and stores.

The *Pandora* then worked her way down the river to Blackstrakes where she received 20 six-pounder carriage guns and four 18-pounder carronades. An impressive armament to be pitted against the 25 mutineers, some of which, it was known, would not resist, and *Bounty* which carried only four "short" 4-pounders. With nearly six times as many men and 12 times the fire power of her prey, *Pandora* might today be considered "a bit of overkill". Her presence in the Pacific would give the Spaniards something to think about.

Pandora arrived at Portsmouth on 17 October and found riding there Admiral Lord Howe's Grand Fleet preparing for war against Spain. Edwards' log entry for 22 October includes a simple statement: " . . . a signal was made for a Court-Martial and for weekly accounts". The court-martial referred to was that of William Bligh to be convened on board HMS *Royal William* anchored nearby. Edwards makes no further mention of the trial, but one can be assured that he took a particular interest in its proceedings and its outcome. It would appear that the relationship between the two men was less than cordial. A notation in the Rev. James Bligh's copy of Bligh's *Narrative* says, "Captain Bligh told me repeatedly that Captain Edwards would never return, as he did not know the navigation of Endeavour Straits". Only Torres, Cook, and Bligh had ever navigated the Straits and the first two were dead. Was this petulance on Bligh's part?

Edwards' formal orders are dated 25 October, three days after the trial. They make no mention of breadfruit, only the capture of Fletcher Christian, the mutineers, and *Bounty*. It is important to note here that on the following day, Thomas Hayward, midshipman of *Bounty*, and having served as a witness at Bligh's court-martial, reported on board *Pandora* as third lieutenant. On the same day, Admiral Cornish's fleet sailed from Portsmouth for the West Indies to prepare for an attack on the Spanish in that part of the world.

A letter (probably of 27 October and incorrectly dated the 24th) from Bligh to Joseph Banks illustrates some of his concerns at this time:

> Dear Sir, I am happy to inform you that on Friday last I was most honourably acquitted respecting the loss of the *Bounty* . . . I came to town on Saturday night, & yesterday morning I waited on Lord Chatham who assured me of promotion as soon as he had been with the King . . . I received your obliging letter of the 4th instant, since which the cause of my not writing to you was the daily suspense I was kept in respecting my tryal . . . There was at Spithead 43 sail of the line — Admiral Cornish was to sail as [of] yesterday with 5 [actually 6] sail besides Frigates . . . The *Pandora*, if they [the Admiralty] don't forget, will sail in the beginning of the Month — she is not fitted or intended to carry any plants . . .

As mentioned, the possibility cannot be discounted that Edwards and *Pandora* may have, at some time, been considered for the second breadfruit mission as an adjunct to the capture of the mutineers. In any event, it would appear that at least Bligh had not been consulted, and something had caused him to make inquiries and forward a specific statement to Banks on that issue. The probability of some animosity between Bligh and Edwards may have inspired *Pandora*'s captain to demonstrate that the *Bounty*'s captain had no monopoly on the recognition and patronage to be derived from a voyage to the Pacific. Indeed, Edwards would have been very remiss not to take advantage of the opportunity.

Pandora departed the coast of England on 7 November and set a course for Tenerife in the Canary Islands. On 18 November, Edwards cleared for action having seen a strange ship of war. It proved to be His Majesty's Sloop *Shark*, Lieutenant Brisac, in quest of Admiral Cornish. Brisac informed Edwards that the dispute with Spain had been amicably settled and that the English fleets were being recalled.

After Tenerife, *Pandora*'s next port of call was Rio de Janeiro at which they arrived on 31 December. It is during their visit here that Edwards' intention to make the voyage into something other than a simple police action begins to surface. Surgeon Hamilton records in his journal:

> I cannot, in words, bestow sufficient panegyric on the laudable exertions of my worthy messmates, Lieutenants Corner and Hayward, for their unremitting zeal in procuring and nursing such plants as might be useful at Otaheitee or the islands we might discover.

This was an activity taken directly from the journals of Cook's voyages and one of particular interest to Banks and, consequently, Bligh.

Having rounded Cape Horn without incident, *Pandora* passed within sight of Easter Island on 4 March 1791. Hamilton says: "We now set the forge to work, and the armourers were busily employed in making knives and iron work to trade with the savages."

Since Magellan had entered the Pacific by the same route in 1525, Europeans had found iron to be their most valuable currency among the Neolithic island cultures. The islanders had three basic commodities to trade for the European treasures; fresh food and water, the favours of their women, and "curiosities" such as exotic seashells and souvenirs of their cultures. The last could make a man either famous or rich on his return to England. It was the collections of Pacific curiosities which had greatly contributed to Banks' rise to prominence in the scientific and social world and, there was a ready and willing market for such things among wealthy collectors of England and Europe.

After logging three other small islands as new discoveries during the next few days, the first being named Ducie's Island after Edwards' patron, *Pandora* dropped anchor in the transparent blue waters of Matavai Bay on the north coast of Tahiti. It was the morning of 23 March. As *Pandora* had slowly worked into the bay, a native paddled off and was taken on board. He brought the news that several of the mutineers were on the island, but that Fletcher Christian and eight others had left some time ago.

Shortly afterwards, another canoe came alongside bearing Joseph Coleman, armourer of the *Bounty*. Coleman was not a true mutineer. During the incident, he, Norman, and McIntosh had attempted to enter the launch with Bligh and the dispossessed crew, but had been stopped by Christian and Bligh had recorded their innocence in the affair.

Coleman informed Edwards that 16 of the mutineers had left the *Bounty* at Tahiti. Of these, two were dead. Churchill and Thompson had lived with a chief in a distant part of the island. Churchill had become *Tyo*, or paramount friend of the chief. Upon the chief's death, by Tahitian custom he had become chief of the district. Thompson, in a jealous rage, had killed Churchill. The revengeful Tahitians had killed Thompson and, later, his skull was brought to Edwards as proof.

At 11.30 that morning, midshipmen Peter Heywood and George Stewart gave themselves up. Heywood had been not quite 17 at the time of the mutiny. Both came from well respected families and Heywood's were acquainted with the Captain. Bligh had treated Heywood as a son on *Bounty* and was tremendously hurt when he mistakenly perceived the young midshipman to be a part of the mutiny. In fact, Heywood's youth and inexperience had left him in an indecisive situation during the chaos of the mutiny.

Edwards' orders, and his own inherent determination to conduct an exemplary mission, allowed him no discretion to make judgments which were the prerogative of higher authority. As a consequence, all of the mutineers, whether they had been cleared by Bligh, or not, were treated equally and without prejudice. They were all guilty until proven innocent by court-martial. He delegated the responsibility of the capture of the prisoners to his officer best qualified to deal with the islanders, third lieutenant Hayward. Their confinement and maintenance was the responsibility of first lieutenant Larkan. As a result, their treatment was undoubtedly harsher than might have been if he had taken more direct responsibility. Also of concern was the fact that many of the islanders were very protective of their mutineer friends. Some had even planned a rescue attempt which Edwards could not allow. As the prisoners came aboard, they were confined in irons below

John Simpson. Peter Heywood, 1812-25? Kindly lent by the National Maritime Museum, London (No.52)

Heywood was one of the mutineers captured by HMS Pandora. He was sentenced to death by the court-martial, but later acquitted, largely due to family influence. In 1792 he inherited £30,000 but remained in the Navy attaining the rank of Captain.

decks and isolated from their islander friends and the crew while the carpenters were set to work constructing a wooden cell on the quarterdeck. This was to be nick-named ''Pandora's Box.''

At three o'clock that afternoon, Richard Skinner, late master's servant and ship's barber of *Bounty*, surrendered himself. The following day, Michael Byrne, a nearly blind fiddler who had been recruited by Bligh merely for his entertainment value, gave himself up.

Before *Pandora*'s arrival, some of the mutineers had been engaged in the construction of a small schooner under the guidance of boatswain's mate James Morrison. The intention was to sail to the north-west coast of America or Batavia in the East Indies and from there make their way back to England. Morrison had previously been a midshipman and was mature and intelligent enough to be accepted as a leader among his fellow outcasts. Edwards received information of the group's intention to sail and dispatched two of *Pandora*'s boats to apprehend them. They were unsuccessful. Once sighted, the schooner soon outdistanced the ship's boats. Morrison's later testimony revealed that the decision of the schooner's crew was to ''not see'' *Pandora*'s boats, but to return to the island and give themselves up of their own volition thus strengthening their plea of innocence.

Once safe from immediate arrest, the schooner did return to the island. Morrison, Norman, and Ellison walked along the beach toward *Pandora*'s

anchorage and gave themselves up. The rest had taken refuge in the mountains.

Edwards again dispatched two boats with a number of armed men to apprehend the remaining mutineers. On 9 April, one boat returned with Hildebrant and McIntosh as prisoners. On the following day, the other boat returned with Burkitt, Milward, Sumner and Muspratt. That made 14 mutineers captured and with Churchill and Thompson dead, only Christian and the eight others on *Bounty* remained to be found.

Pandora remained at Tahiti for 47 days, 18 of which had been spent rounding up the 14 mutineers. The remainder of the time was devoted to the repair of the ship, replenishing supplies of water and food, refitting the small schooner as a tender, and ''refreshing'' the crew. Hamilton writes a very descriptive account of the period. He mentions the collecting of curiosities and breadfruit, the establishment of gardens with the plants brought on *Pandora*, and he also spends some time on a description of the lifestyle and customs of the islanders.

But Edwards' main concern was where next to search for Fletcher Christian and the *Bounty*. Information gathered from some of the prisoners' diaries found on the island and from interviews with them had not produced a convincing answer. Christian had been intentionally circumspect about his eventual destination. He knew that someone would come searching for him.

Pandora and the tender, now named the *Matavia* [Matavai] and manned by master's mate Oliver, midshipman Renouard, and seven other men, sailed from Tahiti on 9 May 1791 to commence a four-month investigation of the most likely Pacific island groups. Only a few things occurred during the unsuccessful search which space allows mentioning here.

On 22 June off Upolu Island in the Samoan Group, *Pandora* and the tender were separated in the darkness. Edwards spent a month here seeking the missing schooner. With great sadness, he reluctantly gave them up for lost. Young Renouard had been the 16 year old son of Edwards' neighbour in Lincolnshire. The lad had desired to go to sea but, because of a speech impediment, his father tried to discourage him. On Edwards' appointment to *Pandora*, he offered to take the boy as one of his servants in the capacity of a clerk where his disability would not pose a problem. When the Admiralty ordered that all officers' servants be discharged, Edwards sought the father's permission and re-enlisted him as midshipman.

Sailing with the prevailing winds and currents, Edwards gradually worked his way westward through the various islands until he determined that he was beyond the area where *Bounty* might be found and the season was getting late for a passage through Endeavour Strait before the north-westerly monsoons came. It was time to give up the search. He had every reason to be contented. He had captured the majority of the mutineers, his crew was perfectly healthy, he had collected breadfruit and curiosities, made new discoveries, and had done his utmost to discover the whereabouts of Christian and *Bounty*. The only task left to achieve was to find a more direct route through Endeavour Strait.

On 14 August in passing an island which is now one of the most southern of the Solomons group, Edwards named it Pitt's Island (Vanikoro Island) in honour of the Prime Minister. Sailing within a mile of the fringing reef, Edwards observed that the smoke of fires was seen indicating that the island was inhabited. What he did not realize was that beneath the waters of that same reef were resting the two wrecks of the Laperouse expedition which had disappeared in 1788 and possibly the last two survivors were then on the island awaiting rescue. By the time the mystery of the Frenchman's disappearance was finally solved 35 years later, it was too late for the survivors and the details of the last months of the Laperouse expedition were lost forever.

Pandora then approached the formidable barrier of Australia's great reef. Finding his way blocked, Edwards turned southwards along the coral wall seeking an entrance. Just before noon on 28 August, a boat was sent to examine an opening in the reef. At 2 o'clock that afternoon (which was now 29 August in the log as shipboard days commenced at midday; in fact, it was the 30th as they had crossed the international dateline), the sailing officer eased the ship in closer. At 4.30 they "hove to" to await the boat. Fifteen minutes later, the boat signalled that they had found a passage through the reef. It was 20 minutes past 7 before the boat was back under the stern of the ship and at that moment *Pandora* struck a submerged reef tearing away her rudder and part of her sternpost. Within five minutes, there were 18 inches of water in the hold and five minutes later, there were four feet. The hands were set to the ship's pumps and three of the mutineers, Coleman, Norman, and McIntosh were released to assist. Others of the crew bailed with buckets at the hatchways, but the leak steadily gained on them and an hour and a half later there were over eight feet of water in the hold. The weather had deteriorated and the ship felt and sounded as if she were pounding herself to pieces on the rock-hard coral. The mutineers, still confined and in darkness, began to panic. Fearful that they would not be given a chance to save themselves if the ship went down, they wrenched their irons off. Learning of this, Edwards had their irons put back on and the guards doubled, threatening to shoot or hang them if they attempted to escape again. Although the situation was undoubtedly a desperate one, it probably appeared to the mutineers worse than it was. Edwards and his entire crew were fully occupied trying to keep the ship afloat and the mutineers were not the only ones who were frightened. However, the reef was no more than 100 yards across and the depth of the water over it, even at low tide, was sufficient to allow the ship to be lifted by each succeeding wave and moved closer to the more protected waters on the lee side. Once there, at least the damaging pounding would cease and there would be a chance to stop the leak.

Two and a half hours after striking the reef, *Pandora* had beaten her way across it into deeper water. The small bower anchor was let go and a cable paid out. Then the best bower anchor was let go directly beneath the ship to steady her. They continued pumping and bailing for the remainder of the night barely keeping the ship afloat until daylight. But, as *Pandora* settled deeper, the leaks increased. The guns were ordered to be thrown overboard to lighten ship, the ship took a heel, and one gun crashed across the deck crushing a man. Another was crushed by a spare topmast falling from its stowage midships. Edwards consulted his officers and they agreed that the ship could not be saved. Supplies were thrown into the boats and everything that would float was cut loose on deck so that when she went down, the crew would have something to cling to.

At this point, Edwards ordered that the prisoners be released from their irons and brought on deck a few at a time. Armourer's mate, Hodges and the ship's corporal entered the cell to release Muspratt, Skinner, and Byrne. The panic was such that Skinner was hauled out of the box with his irons still on and the other two followed him closely. The scuttle was quickly slammed shut and barred before Hodges could get to it and he, in the meantime, removed Morrison's and Stewart's manacles. Morrison begged the master-at-arms to leave the scuttle open, but he had hardly spoken the words when the ship began to sink. The master-at-arms and the sentries rolled over

Robert Batty, after Peter
Heywood. HMS Pandora *in*
the act of foundering.
SLNSW
(No.49)
The original drawing was
done by one of the
mutineers, Peter Heywood
and shows the Pandora
going down after it struck
the Reef.

the side and the prisoners could see through the stern ports that Captain Edwards was swimming towards the pinnace. The bow of the ship was underwater as far as the mainmast and the sea was beginning to flow in on them. Boatswain's mate Moulter scrambled onto the roof of the cell, pulled the bar securing the scuttle through the coamings and threw the hatch cover aside before he leapt into the sea. All managed to get out of the cell except Hildebrant as the ship went down. Morrison saw a large wooden gangway burst to the surface with Muspratt clinging to it. It crashed down on the heads of several men in the water, including Stewart and Sumner, and sent them to the bottom. The top of "Pandora's Box" had floated off and on it were Heywood, Burkitt, Coleman, and first lieutenant Larkan. Heywood grabbed a nearby plank and began swimming towards one of the boats and Morrison followed his example. Hamilton records: "The cries of the men drowning in the water was at first awful in the extreme: but as they sank and became faint, they died away by degrees."

After the boats took up as many survivors as could be found, they landed on a small sand cay about three miles from the wreck and began to take stock of their situation. A roll call revealed that 89 of the ship's crew and 10 of the mutineers had survived. Thirty-one of the ship's company and Hildebrant, Stewart, Sumner, and Skinner had been lost with the ship. Skinner and Hildebrant had still been wearing their wrist irons.

Tents were made of the boat's sails for the officers and crew, but the prisoners were kept at the other end of the cay and not allowed any shelter from the intense tropical sun. It would seem to be an act of senseless cruelty and may have been the decision of lieutenant Hayward. This would be the second time these mutineers had been the cause of his having to suffer the unpleasant trials of an open boat voyage to Timor. The white sand of the cay can be hot enough to blister bare feet and the reflected sun's rays will cause extreme sunburn within a very short time. The mutineers had been confined in the dark, sweltering cell for five months. They had few articles of clothing and their skin was soft. To try to find some relief, they buried themselves in the hot sand during the heat of the day but even so, they had their skin "flea'd from head to foot".

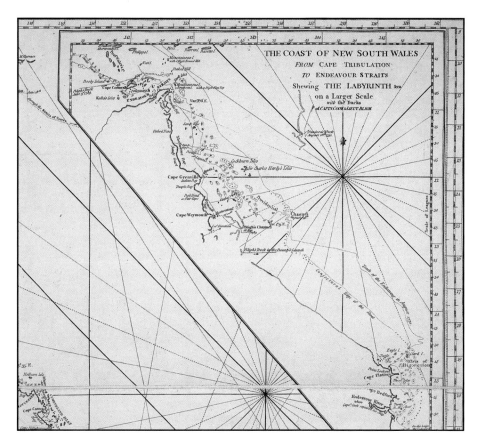

Laurie and Whittle. A New Chart of the Eastern Coast of New Holland ... 1798 (i.e. c.1800). SLNSW (No.50)

A chart showing the reef where the Pandora foundered on 28 August 1791 on the treacherous Great Barrier Reef, north of where Cook's Endeavour went aground in 1770

Two days were spent preparing the boats for the attempt to reach Timor and on 31 August they departed "Escape Key". They were now inside the outer line of the barrier and only small isolated reefs were in their path to Endeavour Straits which lay about 120 miles to the north-west. Once through the Straits, it was another 1,000 miles of open sea to Timor.

The events of the next 16 days were highlighted by an encounter with hostile natives, hunger and debilitating thirst. On arrival at Timor, Edwards arranged passage on a Dutch vessel as far as Batavia for his surviving crew, the mutineers, and a group of escaped convicts from Port Jackson who were now placed in his charge. The vessel called into Samarang for repairs. To Edwards' delight, they found anchored there the missing tender and all its crew. At Batavia, Edwards divided his entourage among four Dutch East Indiamen and at the Cape of Good Hope transferred most of them to HMS *Gorgon* for the voyage to England where they arrived on 19 June 1792.

On 10 September, Captain Edwards, together with his officers, appeared before a court-martial held on board HMS *Hector* to answer for the loss of *Pandora*. Edwards submitted a written statement describing the circumstances of the wreck. Lieutenants Larkan and Corner and other officers swore to the truth of the Captain's account. The court then found Edwards, his officers, and men without blame for the loss of the ship.

Two days later, nearly three years and five months after the mutiny, the trial of the 10 mutineers began on board HMS *Duke*. Bligh was not able to attend. He was somewhere in the Pacific on his second breadfruit voyage.

During their confinement, the prisoners had worked hard to prepare their defence against the charges. Heywood carried on a copious correspondence with his widowed mother and three devoted sisters. Through their efforts,

and those of his uncle, Commodore Pasley and his brother, all of their best family connections were brought to bear on Heywood's case. Even Captain Edwards tried to serve him before the trial. In a letter written to Mr C. Christian, he refers to Heywood as an "unfortunate young man" and goes on to say: "I apprehend he did not take an active part against Mr Bligh . . ." and, "it is greatly to be lamented that youth through their own indiscretion, or bad example, should be involved in such difficulties, and bring ignominy on themselves, and distress to their friends."

The trial lasted for six days. As could be expected, Coleman, Norman, McIntosh, and the blind fiddler Byrne, were acquitted. Ellison, Burkitt, Millward, Muspratt, Morrison and Heywood were sentenced to death. The court, however, recommended the King's Mercy for Morrison and Heywood. It was not until 17 October that they were advised that the King had granted them his "free and unconditional pardon". Muspratt's case was discharged on a legal technicality and he was given his freedom. On 29 October 1792, the three remaining men were publicly hanged on board HMS *Brunswick*.

When Bligh had sailed on 3 August 1791 for his second breadfruit voyage, he was still basking in the approbation of all England. On his return at the conclusion of his voyage on 7 August 1793, he found his reception considerably cooler than he had expected. During his absence, more had been made public about the *Bounty* voyage than he might have wished. The trial of the mutineers had attracted widespread public interest. The witnesses, such as Fryer, Cole and Purcell, and the mutineers, had not been reticent in their mention of some of Bligh's shortcomings.

Even Sir Joseph Banks had cause to have second thoughts about Bligh's veracity. Morrison had completed his account after the trial while awaiting the King's consideration. There is evidence to suggest that Heywood at least read the manuscript and made suggestions for changes. Morrison had then sent a copy to Rev. W. Howell on the Isle of Wight. Howell wrote to Captain Molesworth Phillips on 25 November 1792 stating that Morrison's manuscript was ready to publish, but that he would send it to Banks, if it was desired, as he considered that the contents might be detrimental to the reputation of certain officers. Indeed, Morrison, and by association Heywood, had written things which could damage the careers of several officers, including Edwards. Howell's letter and presumably a copy of the manuscript which was later passed on to Bligh were sent to Banks. It would appear that publication may have been stopped by Banks' intervention, or possibly at the desire of the First Lord. On 5 January 1793, Banks had reason to write to Lord Chatham in defence of Bligh's qualities. It would also appear that Banks wrote to *Bounty*'s midshipman Hallett desiring certain information about the mutineers while Bligh was away. Was he seeking verification of some disturbing details?

On his return, Bligh complained to Banks of Lord Chatham's "unaccountable conduct". Lieutenant Portlock, Bligh's second captain commanding the *Assistant*, gained an immediate interview with the First Lord, whereas Bligh, the expedition commander, was kept waiting for several days. On being discharged from the *Providence* on 7 September, Bligh was placed on half-pay and was to remain unemployed until 29 April 1795.

During 1793, surgeon George Hamilton published his journal of the voyage of *Pandora*. Although the slender volume contains some mistakes of fact, certain passages have been taken nearly word-for-word from Captain Edwards' manuscript account which was not published until 1915. Collaboration between the Captain and his surgeon would also explain the

Thomas Phillips. Sir Joseph Banks, c.1808-1809. SLNSW (No.11)

Sir Joseph Banks, the foremost natural scientist of his day and long-serving President of the Royal Society, London, was the driving force behind the expedition led by Bligh to collect breadfruit trees to transplant in the West Indies. Banks had visited Tahiti with Cook's First Voyage in 1769.

glossing-over of certain incidents and the complete omission of others. Hamilton's writing is an obvious attempt to describe *Pandora*'s voyage in the genre of science and discovery. His forthright description of the lascivious customs of the Tahitians was bound to draw criticism and attract for him the label of ''licentious''.

On 30 October 1793, Bligh wrote to Banks and discussed the attacks on his reputation by various people in his absence and refuted statements made in Morrison's unpublished journal which he had obviously read.

But that was not to be the end of it. In 1794, Edward Christian, brother of Fletcher, published a portion of the minutes of the mutineers' court-martial with an appendix defending his brother. The appendix included condemning statements supposedly made by various participants of the *Bounty* incident. Bligh was prompted to publish an answer to the allegations in the December 1794 issue of *The British Critic*. A detail worthy of note is that Bligh's ''Answer'' included a statement supposedly made by Coleman on

Artefacts from the wreck of HMS Pandora, *1791. Kindly lent by the Queensland Museum, Brisbane (No.47)*

Since 1983, the Maritime Archaeology Section of the Queensland Museum has been excavating the wreck of the Pandora *on the northern tip of the Great Barrier Reef, off Cape York. Ship's equipment, personal possessions of the crew and Tahitian curiosities collected as memorabilia have so far been uncovered.*

Bligh's behalf. It is signed with an "X" and captioned "Coleman's Mark". A copy of Coleman's own written account of the early part of *Bounty*'s voyage had been forwarded to Banks. It was not the writings of a man who could not sign his own name.

One hundred and eighty-six years after the wreck of *Pandora*, a group of scuba divers with the assistance of the Royal Australian Air Force, relocated the ship's final resting place. She lies in 120 feet of water buried in a gently sloping sandy bottom between two coral reefs. On the surface of the seabed can be seen the anchor which was used to steady the ship, the fluke of what is probably the *Bounty* anchor abandoned by Christian and recovered by Edwards at Tahiti, cannon, the ship's galley stove, and parts of the ship's pumps at which the crew had worked so hard to save *Pandora* and their own lives.

Since 1983, the Queensland Museum's Maritime Archaeology Section has organized three eight-week seasons of excavation on the site. To date, perhaps 5 per cent of the wreck has been explored and recorded. By using an electronic instrument which sends sound waves down through the seabed, it has been determined that *Pandora*'s remains beneath the sand are comparable to those of England's *Mary Rose*.

Apart from the usual items found on most shipwrecks, some relics of great importance have been found on *Pandora* which will help us to better understand one of the most significant periods of Pacific and, indeed, world history. Particularly noteworthy is a collection of medical instruments and belongings which can be identified with surgeon Hamilton. But of even more importance is a collection of "curiosities" which may comprise part of what Edwards submitted a claim to the Admiralty for on his return to England. His account was for £200 which was a great deal of money in those times.

Pandora was equipped and provisioned much the same as, and in some respects better than, the expeditions of Cook and Bligh. Of all the 18th century voyages to the Pacific, only the two wrecks of Laperouse and the wreck of *Pandora* will ever provide us with the minute details which give substance to written history. Of these wrecks, *Pandora* has the most potential. Unfortunately, the excavation of *Pandora* has been halted due to the lack of financial support.

In 1986, the most emotive discovery of all was made. Buried in the stern section of *Pandora*'s wreck was a human skeleton.

Ronald A Coleman is Curator of Maritime History and Archaeology at Queensland Museum, Australia.

TURNING A MUTINY INTO LEGEND

Gavin Kennedy

Of the 46 men and boys who sailed on *Bounty* from Spithead on 23 December 1787, two died before the mutiny (one of blood poisoning, the other of alcoholism), 10 were murdered after the mutiny (by each other, or by Polynesians), four drowned while prisoners, three were hanged (another three were pardoned), and five died from disease or the after-effects of the open boat voyage. (Details of the entire *Bounty* crew, including those who deserted before she sailed, are provided in D. Bonner Smith's article, ''Some Remarks about the Mutiny of the *Bounty*'', *The Mariner's Mirror*, vol 23, no 2, 1937).

For the survivors, the mutiny disrupted but did not destroy their careers. William Bligh was promoted to post captain and died a Vice-Admiral of the Blue in 1817; midshipmen Thomas Hayward and John Hallett were promoted lieutenants, but later drowned in sea tragedies; midshipman Peter Heywood, found guilty of mutiny but pardoned, rose to post captain's rank, and retired after a distinguished career; John Fryer, *Bounty*'s master, rose to become a master of the 1st rate, and served at the battles of St Vincent and Copenhagen; Robert Tinkler, ''midshipman'' (and Fryer's brother-in-law) became a lieutenant and commander (and also served at Copenhagen); and James Morrison, boatswain's mate, drowned in 1807 while gunner on Admiral Troubridge's flagship, HMS *Blenheim*.

The mutiny, however, put at risk the reputations of all concerned from the moment the world heard what had happened from 4 am of that fateful morning, 28 April 1789. That the Admiralty was bound to be interested in what had happened on any of the King's ships was predictable — it could be concerned about events more trivial than mutinies, as any ship's log shows — but that the world continues to be fascinated by the mutiny is a matter of some curiosity, given the relatively unimportant mission *Bounty* was engaged on and the tumultuous events then happening in Europe and North America. Moreover, that the men involved, particularly William Bligh and Fletcher Christian, can excite such passions after 200 years, that supporters and detractors mobilize behind one view or another of those involved, that pamphlets and letters of abuse cross the globe, with personal motives questioned — indeed reputations rubbished — and dark allusions made to personal dishonesty and scholarly ethics, is probably a greater mystery than the causes of the mutiny itself.

The literature about the fatal voyage of HMS *Bounty* is already vast, and there is no sign that it has ceased growing. True, more is known about the men and the mutiny now than at any time previously, but gaps remain in the historical record, and tantalizing hints of hidden literary treasures

occasionally surface. Not least among the latter is the complete absence to date of any material directly written by Fletcher Christian himself (his only known signature is among some *Bounty* papers in the Mitchell Library in Sydney). We know that he sent letters to his family from the Cape in May 1788, before the mutiny, but no trace of them has been found (his letters to his brother, Charles, would be of special interest). We know that he destroyed some of his papers immediately before the mutiny (in case they were used as evidence against him if he failed?) If Christian took advantage of the opportunities he had after the mutiny to record his version of why he mutinied — he had charge of all *Bounty*'s writing instruments and papers (including boxes of Bligh's lifetime collection of navigation and sailing books and personal records) — he hid his efforts too well, or too carelessly. Hence, we have to rely on second-hand reports of his reasons from Peter Heywood and James Morrison, who were among Christian's party that stayed behind at Tahiti, and John Adams (aka Alexander Smith), the last survivor of the bloody murders on Pitcairn.

For the other figures in the mutiny, the literary record is extensive despite the gaps. Some of the manuscript logs and journals are accessible to the public, without the necessity of expensive trips to the libraries where the originals are preserved in London and Sydney — even highly priced special and facsimile editions of logs and journals still incite a seemingly inexhaustible market for *Bountyana*. In addition, a number of books is also available, for much the same reason as with the manuscripts, and can be found in good public libraries: The *Bounty*'s Log has been published in two limited editions: the first was transcribed and edited in two volumes by Owen Rutter in the Golden Cockerel Press series in 1937: *The Log of the Bounty, being Lieutenant William Bligh's Log of the Proceedings of His Majesty's Armed vessel 'Bounty', on a voyage to the South Seas to take the breadfruit from the Society Islands to the West Indies, now published for the first time from the*

Francois Peron and Charles Lesueur. Vue de Coupang, Timour (View of Kupang, Timor) 1801. SLNSW (No.31)

Charles Benezach. Lieut. Bligh and his crew of the ship Bounty *hospitably received by the Governor of Timor, 1791. SLNSW (No.32)*

Bligh and the crew of the Bounty's longboat are seen arriving at the Dutch settlement of Timor on 14 July 1791 after their heroic voyage. When the engraving was published in London, Bligh was enjoying great acclaim as a popular hero.

'Just before Sunrise Mr
Christian & the Master at
Arms & several others came
into my Cabbin while I was
fast asleep, and seizing me
tyed my hands with a Cord
& threatned instant death if
I made the least noise'
Entry for 28 April 1789,
the morning of the mutiny
on HMS Bounty, from the
private log of William
Bligh.
Bligh's grandson, W.R.
Bligh donated the logbook to
the Library in 1902.
SLNSW (No. 27)

Page from the account of
James Morrison, the
Bounty's Boatswain's mate.
Morrison remained with
Christian on the Bounty,
returned to Tahiti and was
arrested there by Captain
Edward Edwards.

Morrison's narrative presents
a different view of the
mutiny to that of Bligh and
is highly critical of his
command. After Morrison's
death in 1807, this account
was plundered by Peter
Heywood (1825), Sir John
Barrow (1831) and Lady
Belcher (1870) in their
attacks on Bligh's
reputation. Their widely
circulated opinions which
present Bligh as a
tyrannically cruel man have
remained unchallenged
in popular belief.
SLNSW (No. 46)

manuscript in the Admiralty records; the second was a facsimile of the official log, published as a limited edition in 1975 by Genesis (London) as: *The Log of H.M.S.* Bounty. A popularly priced transcript of the log was published in 1978 as *Mutiny!! Aboard H M Armed Transport 'Bounty' in 1789 by R.M. Bowker and by Lt. William Bligh, RN in his official log (with illustrations including real charts)*. A facsimile and transcript of Bligh's pocket-size journal which he kept in the open boat was published in 1986 by the National Library of Australia as a limited edition: *The Bligh Notebook: Facsimile and Transcription: 'Rough Account — Lieutenant Wm Bligh's voyage in the* Bounty's *Launch from the ship to Tofoa & from thence to Timor, 28 April to 14 June 1789'. With a draft list of the* Bounty *mutineers*, edited by John Bach (a popularly priced edition of this interesting literary treasure was published subsequently in the United States).

Bligh's own versions of the mutiny, first published in 1790 and 1792, have seen numerous modern editions in several languages. Partly, this has been encouraged by the interest in Bligh as one of the early, and typically controversial, Governors of the Colony of New South Wales (where he suffered another mutiny), which has motivated various Australian libraries to collect almost anything connected with Bligh. Many of the important manuscripts of witnesses to the mutiny have also been published within the past 50 years, while those who are able to visit the Public Record Office at Kew, or the Mitchell Library in Sydney, will find most of the rest of the material needed to form a view of the men and the mutiny.

Views about Bligh and the men on board HMS *Bounty* have changed more than once over the two centuries since his second-in-command placed him under armed arrest and put him over the side into one of the ship's boats. To a large extent, these public moods follow the publication of books and

Henry Roberts. Matavai Bay, Tahiti, 1773. SLNSW (No.1)

articles asserting this or that version of each man's motives. Indeed, it was Bligh's own effort to explain the mutiny to the wider public that prevented it from becoming merely another footnote in the history of the Royal Navy.

Bligh's *Narrative of the Mutiny on board His Majesty's Ship* Bounty; *and the subsequent voyage of part of the crew in the ship's boat from Tofoa, one of the Friendly islands, to Timor, a Dutch Settlement in the East Indies* (1790) gave his version of the events from the mutiny to the successful conclusion of the open boat voyage to the Dutch East Indies. This version, it must be said, was less than candid.

In journalistic terms, Bligh had a story to tell, especially after surviving the rigours of the open boat voyage, but he also had another motive: to explain why a mutiny had occurred on his ship, and why he was unable to prevent it, or having failed to prevent it, why he, or some of the loyal men in the crew, were unable to put it down. His career, if not his pride, depended on how convincing was the explanation he gave to the Admiralty and to the wider public.

Certainly, Bligh's overt behaviour the night before the mutiny supports his later claim to have been totally surprised by it — he slept without a sentry outside his cabin; he was unarmed, having given his pistols to John Fryer, the master; and he had not secured the key to the arm's chest, having delegated that task to Fryer, who in turn had delegated it to Joseph Coleman, the armourer. Thus, Bligh showed that he had no idea that a mutiny threatened, because otherwise he would have taken steps to prevent it. This led him to imply, therefore, that the men who mutinied were able to do so only because they had engaged in a deeply hidden conspiracy. But this left the question: why did Christian mutiny? If Bligh swore that there was no obvious cause for the men to mutiny arising from his own behaviour as captain, he had to have a convincing alternative to account for the fact that nevertheless they had done so. He found this in the spectre of sex:

> It will very naturally be asked, what could be the reason for such a revolt? in answer to which, I can only conjecture that the mutineers had assured themselves of a more happy life amongst the Otaheiteans, than they could possibly have in England; which, joined to some female connections, have most probably been the principal cause of the whole transaction.

That there might have been a sexual motivation among some of the men who mutinied, and in some of those who were none too zealous in putting it down, is plausible, but this does not explain Christian's behaviour (nor does Bligh claim that it does — he did not allude directly to Christian's motives in the above explanation, referring instead to the motives of ''the mutineers'' in general). That some of the men had formed sexual attachments during their five month's stay in Tahiti is undisputed (Heywood, Stewart and Morrison, for example), as is the probability that some of the mutineers may have been seduced by their recent memories of Tahitian women into seizing the opportunity of Christian's mutiny to return to them, undeterred even by the gruesome punishments of the Articles of War for mutiny.

While not explaining Christian's behaviour, Bligh's 1790 *Narrative* provided an explanation for the mutiny that did not require, if it was accepted, further enquiry into Bligh's general conduct and fitness for command. Men regularly deserted Royal Navy ships, and not always in places as attractive as Tahiti. Some did it to escape from naval service or to avoid punishment; many for other reasons unconnected with the way they were managed by their commanding officers. The punishment, if caught, was severe — death or a heavy flogging. That seamen would run for sex and a life of plenty (however illusory in fact) was plausible and, in the absence of contrary evidence, it absolved Bligh from public ignominy. The fact that the sequel to the mutiny was the open boat voyage across the Pacific more than justified the credibility of his claims to have been a good commander who was the innocent victim of a dastardly plot by base men led by base officers. There is no doubt that this is how Bligh saw the mutiny and his role in it. He was never aware of how hurtful or destructive his manner could be to those whom he commanded, particularly those of whom he had the greatest hopes.

The impact of Bligh's *Narrative* on the reading public was considerable, and in so far as he expressed the same convincing views to the Admiralty, and to the relatives of those who had mutinied, he was assured of no repercussions on his career. But, if it was a conscious effort on his part to mislead, if only by omission, it was flawed in one key respect: that there were other survivors who had been witnesses to the transactions he had made public.

For the moment at least, Bligh's version swept all before it. His court-martial for the loss of *Bounty* acquitted him of any dereliction of duty, and a grateful Sovereign had him promoted from lieutenant to the coveted rank of post captain (the Admiralty having to pull some awkward procedural strings for this to take effect).

John Fryer, the *Bounty*'s master, was one potentially hostile witness to Bligh's version of events. He had been much criticised by Bligh during the voyage, mainly on grounds of his alleged professional misconduct. Bligh's personal journal and log (preserved in the Mitchell Library, Sydney), written before the mutiny, contains numerous references to the alleged failures of the master. None of these was made public by Bligh, nor were they included in the official log he deposited at the Admiralty on his return (preserved in the Public Record Office, Kew). A possible explanation for these omissions lies in quarrels Bligh had with his master about his expense books. John Fryer, with Bligh in the open boat, was refused a copy of Bligh's log of the voyage and "therefore in my own Defence I am obliged to write the best my memory will allow me". And write he did. The fact that he wrote in his own "defence" echoes his fears that he was vulnerable to Bligh exacting professional revenge on him once the *Bounty* affair died down.

Fryer's account of the boat voyage was written after Bligh's *Narrative*. In it he gives a different version of the events in the open boat, largely playing-down Bligh's presentation of himself as the sole source of the success of that dangerous journey. Whatever Fryer's motives, his original manuscript account was not published until 1934, and then only as a limited edition by Owen Rutter (editor) in the Golden Cockerel Press series: *The Voyage of the* Bounty*'s Launch, as related in William Bligh's Despatch to the Admiralty and The Journal of John Fryer*. Rutter followed this limited edition with another in the same series in 1939: *John Fryer of the* Bounty: *Notes on his Career Written By his Daughter Mary Ann*. In 1979 Genesis published a contemporary transcript of Fryer's original account, edited by Stephen Walters, as *The Voyage of the* Bounty *Launch: John Fryer's Narrative*.

Fryer's explanation for the mutiny contradicted Bligh's: "from what they [the mutineers] said I suppose they did not like their Captain". Pointedly, he also denied that Christian had a specific female friend while at Tahiti, and suggested that the treatment the boat party received when ashore at Tofoa (where John Norton was murdered) was in revenge for Bligh's treatment of some islanders at nearby Annamooka.

Fryer's 1790 manuscript made the first reference to the "coconut" incident the day before the mutiny, which suggests that all was not as tranquil on

George Tobin. The Observatory — Point Venus, Otahytey, 1792. SLNSW (No.118)

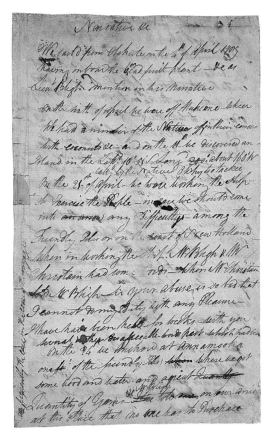

Above

The opening page of John Fryer's narrative of the mutiny on H.M.S. Bounty. John Fryer joined the Bounty as Master. He quarrelled fiercely with Bligh during the voyage following the mutiny. His account of the longboat voyage attempts to lessen Bligh's achievement by revealing errors in navigation. Fryer claimed that Bligh overstated the difficulties of the voyage and deliberately downgraded the possession of adequate navigational instruments. SLNSW (No. 40)

Above right
Gaetano Calleyo. John Fryer, c.1807. SLNSW (No.37)

Fryer, the Master of the Bounty, sailed with Bligh in the longboat voyage. He failed to receive any further promotion and remained in the rank of Master until his death in 1817.

Bounty as Bligh evidently believed, or as he portrayed in his *Narrative*. There had been a row over allegations that members of the crew during the night had helped themselves to some of the coconuts which were stored on deck (it was a hot night and men may have quenched their thirst from the coconuts strewn around the deck). Bligh, in his dual role as captain and purser, intended these to be issued during the voyage as part of the crew's rations. He believed that the men had stolen some of these nuts and that the officers had either been neglectful or in collusion with the thieves. In the row that followed, Fryer states that Bligh demanded of each officer that they account for their stores of nuts and threatened the men that if the thieves were not found the yam allowance would be cut from 1 1/2 lbs to 3/4 lb per day. Interestingly, Fryer, writing in 1790, only mentions one officer by name, Edward Young, midshipman, and does not mention Christian at all. Yet, in the next four years, the coconut incident came to play an increasing central role as the explanation for Christian's mutiny.

Fryer had clashed with Bligh throughout the voyage. In October 1788, after leaving Adventure Bay (in modern Tasmania) Fryer refused to sign the ship's expense books. Bligh bullied Fryer into signing the books and entered details of Fryer's act of dissent in his personal journal and log. There were other incidents between them at Tahiti before the mutiny (and Bligh recorded them, perhaps with a view to preferring charges against Fryer after the voyage). At Sourabaya, Dutch East Indies, in September 1789 after the open boat voyage, which had been occasioned by several rows between them, Fryer was again in trouble with Bligh. According to Bligh, Fryer and others had milled around the deck in a "tumultuous manner", and Bligh had them arrested by the Dutch authorities. If Bligh had hopes of court-martialling

Fryer on the serious charge of open defiance, perhaps even mutinous assembly, they were soon extinguished in this mysterious incident. Bligh fully reported his version of what happened, including details of Fryer's gross insubordination, in his personal journal and log, but in the official log, presented to the Admiralty, he made no reference to the "tumult" at Sourabaya, merely providing a description of the Dutch settlement as "one of the most pleasant places I ever saw".

Bluntly, Fryer claimed he had evidence that Bligh had fiddled his expenses at Coupang in Timor (as with the expense books at Adventure Bay?) He reported his evidence to the Dutch officials who passed on to Bligh the substance of Fryer's charges. These included a list of the prices Bligh claimed to have paid to Dutch merchants for subsistence and the fitting out of the vessel he had purchased, and what Fryer claimed was the actual price list for these same items given to Fryer by the Dutch authorities at Coupang (it is possible that the merchants reported to the authorities lower prices than they charged Bligh to avoid the local sales tax, thus causing a discrepancy). Bligh certainly fumed about his "honour" and berated the Dutch to see the "villainy" of Fryer in trying to entrap his commanding officer. Negotiations continued, however, and the outcome was that Fryer apologized in writing to Bligh. But the apology has to be set beside the fact that Bligh did not make any charges against Fryer at the court-martial for the loss of the *Bounty*, and exercized his prerogative to refrain from making any negative references to Fryer in the official log. Whatever he agreed with Fryer (under the duress of the evidence against him, or because he was advised that it would be unseemly to court-martial his second-in-command?), he court-martialled William Purcell, the irascible ship's carpenter, with whom he had clashed on numerous occasions (the court found the charges in part proved and reprimanded him). However, Fryer, in return perhaps for Bligh's restraint, or because it would damage his career, did not raise any criticism of Bligh when invited to do so by the court-martial.

While both men stuck to their alleged agreement in respect of the court-martial, they certainly did not do more than this. Bligh refused Fryer a reference when Captain Riou asked him for one in 1790, and Fryer, while refraining from public criticism of Bligh, not only wrote his journal for private circulation in 1790 (smarting from Bligh's refusal of a reference?) but also collaborated extensively with Professor Edward Christian (Fletcher's brother) in 1794 to make public certain aspects of Bligh's style of command, of *Bounty* in general, and his treatment of Fletcher Christian in particular.

Meanwhile, Bligh had left on his second breadfruit voyage in HMS *Providence*, and had handed over the editing of a fuller version of the *Bounty* voyage to his friend, Captain, later Admiral, James Burney. This appeared in 1792 as: *A Voyage to the South Seas, undertaken by command of His Majesty, for the purpose of Conveying the Bread-Fruit Tree to the West Indies, in His Majesty's Ship the* Bounty, *commanded by Lieutenant William Bligh*. This gave an account of the voyage prior to the mutiny and repeated the 1790 account of the mutiny from the *Narrative*. Like its predecessor, the *Voyage* has been published many times, including facsimiles of the original 1794 edition (for example one was published by Hutchinson in Australia in 1979) plus numerous paperback editions. Closely following the official versions of *Bounty*'s log, the *Voyage* contains a great deal of interesting material on the customs and culture of the Tahitians. This has given Bligh a reputation as a contributor to the social anthropology of the unique cultures of Tahitian society at the time of their first contacts with Europeans (a role also accorded to James Morrison, boatswain's mate, from the accounts he gave in his

George Tobin. Point Venus — Island of Otahytey, 1792. SLNSW (No.118)

Journal from his long stay on Tahiti after the mutiny). But if Bligh had hopes that the mutiny would fade into the background and that he would continue with his career as a navigator in the steps of Captain James Cook, he was to be sadly disappointed on his return to Britain in 1793.

In Bligh's absence, the Royal Navy had captured the survivors of Christian's party who had been left behind in Tahiti in 1789, and had brought them home for trial (less the four who drowned in the sinking of HMS *Pandora* in 1791). Whatever crimes the men had committed they were entitled to a fair trial from the Admiralty, and they could rely on the firm support of their families irrespective of their guilt or innocence. That some of the men had more influence than others, and had greater family resources at their disposal to see that a conviction was made more difficult, only reflects the social structure of the 18th century. With some of the mutineers still at

William Bligh. The small blue Paroquet of Otaheite . . . 1791-1793, SLNSW (No.121)

Like many naval officers, Bligh was a competent amateur artist who drew fauna, flora and views of the exotic species and places encountered en route. From the sketchbook of 58 watercolours illustrating the Second Breadfruit Voyage.

William Bligh. Mother Careys Chicken ... of Otaheite, 1791-1793, SLNSW (No.121)

large, including the leader, Fletcher Christian, there was also the possibility that the precedents set at this first trial might be applied at a second, or third, trial should other mutineers be captured. Full details of the trial, including transcripts of the evidence for the prosecution and the defence, were published in 1931 by Owen Rutter (editor), *The Court-Martial of the "Bounty Mutineers"*, in the Notable British Trials series.

The prosecution had Bligh's sworn testimonies, the evidence of the court-martial of Bligh and the men who returned with him, and the evidence of those who had returned and who were still in England in 1793. Bligh was not expected back until 1794. The defence could either press to postpone the court-martial until Bligh returned, or press for its early opening before he did so. Which to favour depended on what view was taken of Bligh's likely stance on the guilt or innocence of individuals. He had cleared four men — Joseph Coleman, armourer; Thomas McIntosh, carpenter's mate; Charles Norman, carpenter's mate; and Michael Byrne, seaman (actually a semi-blind fiddler) — of complicity in the mutiny, in his logs and in his publications. They were safe with Bligh's testimony and might have preferred a postponement. Others were less certain of their fate. By implication, all others left on board were mutineers, but some of them, such as Peter Heywood and James Morrison, had hopes of a defence that they were held on board against their will.

James Morrison, boatswain's mate, was a man of more than average intelligence and scholarly inclination. He had been a midshipman for a short period before joining *Bounty* as boatswain's mate. His position on board in no way reflected his abilities and he set these abilities to work to save his life and to expose Bligh's unfitness for command. His literary contributions to the *Bounty* story are preserved in the Mitchell Library, Sydney, and consist of

'Knowing then my own Dear Betsy, I have lost the Bounty'

The first page of William Bligh's letter to his wife, Betsy, describing the mutiny on H.M.S. Bounty. The letter is written from Timor and dated 19 August 1789. Bligh felt compelled to write to his wife lest he die without explaining his version of the mutiny to her. SLNSW (No. 34)

two manuscripts, one entitled 'Memorandums and Particulars respecting the Bounty and her Crew' and the other, known as, 'Morrison's Journal'. The Memorandums manuscript is a copy of the original (now lost) and was presented to the Mitchell Library by one of Bligh's descendants. It was written by Morrison during his confinement with the other prisoners on HMS Hector during September-October 1792. It consists of a short critical account of life on Bounty under Bligh, plus a sharp criticism, in the form of an open letter, of his life as a prisoner on Pandora, and afterwards, under Captain Edward Edwards (an altogether more ferocious disciplinarian than Bligh). The Journal is a more ambitious project, consisting of 382 pages in Morrison's own handwriting, giving a full account of the voyage under Bligh, the mutiny, and the aftermath, first under Christian and then in Tahiti while awaiting the Royal Navy's inevitable search for the mutineers. It was written after Morrison's release (he had been pardoned for mutiny by the King on the court's recommendation) during November 1792 and early spring 1793. Originally it had a Tahitian vocabulary (possibly compiled with or by Peter Heywood) attached, but this is now lost.

The Memorandum's manuscript was circulated among influential public figures after the trial and conviction of the mutineers in September 1792. Its purpose was to secure a pardon for Morrison and Heywood, and perhaps a commutation of the death sentences for the others. While no excuse was possible for mutiny — a man could be convicted for failing to overthrow a mutiny — Morrison intended to show that the man responsible for the mutiny occurring, and, by his earlier conduct, failing to inspire anybody to overthrow it once it had begun, was Lieutenant William Bligh. He did this by reporting incidents that showed that Bligh was a bad commander; alleged misuse of his powers as purser (poor food, fiddled accounts, small rations, theft of some cheese); of having numerous rows with his officers (he details the public dissent of Fryer over the signing of the expense books, his quarrels with Purcell, his dispute with Christian at Annamooka and his row about the coconuts the day before the mutiny). In short, he presents a different picture of the voyage from the one in Bligh's Narrative and Voyage.

That this helped to influence the court is seen in its recommendation of Heywood and Morrison for pardon (though this recommendation was not unconnected with the fact that Heywood had a relative by marriage, Captain Albermarle Bertie, among the officers of the court and could draw on men of considerable influence, such as Commodore Pasley to speak informally to the other members and to the Admiralty, as well as having inherited a sizeable fortune while a prisoner). These efforts, verbally and in writing, plus the evidence that emerged in the trial itself certainly turned official opinion against Bligh, not least because it exposed his own publications, which detail the many innovative and humane changes he made to the management of a ship on a voyage of discovery, to the charge that they were in error, at the very least by omission, and, more damagingly, perhaps also by deceit.

Sir Joseph Banks, the leading botanist and influential friend of the King, read Morrison's Memorandums and passed a copy to Bligh, on his return, for his comments. These Bligh made in a number of letters to Banks (some of which with some detailed notes are preserved in the Mitchell Library under Remarks on Morrison's Journal). These were published in 1937 as a limited edition by Owen Rutter (editor) in the Golden Cockerel Press series: Bligh's Voyage in the Resource and his Remarks on Morrison's Journal. Bligh survived Morrison's criticisms, largely because they had such a restricted circulation at the time, and because his defence of his conduct to Sir Joseph Banks and others, in naval disciplinary terms, was robust. The Memorandums circulated

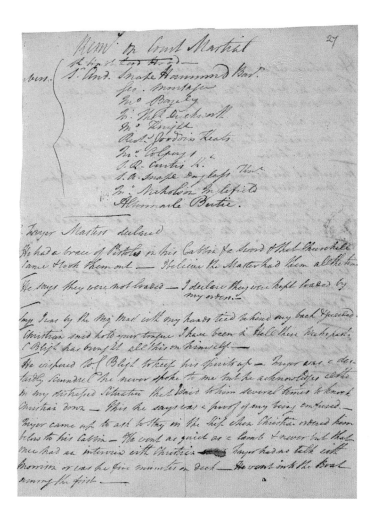

'Rems [Remarks] on Court
Martial'
Notes by William Bligh
concerning the court-martial
of the mutineers.
SLNSW (No. 54)

for a short while, but were not published and Morrison's larger *Journal*
remained almost unknown except to a few people, largely missionaries,
whose interest was confined to the information about Tahiti and its customs
and language, rather than to the events on *Bounty*. However, some of the
criticisms of Bligh in Morrison's manuscripts appeared in 1820-21 (Bligh died
in 1817) in the *Sailor's Magazine and Naval Miscellany*, under the title: 'The
Authentic history of the mutineers of the *Bounty*'.

By the 1820s, Peter Heywood had possession of Morrison's Journal (how
he acquired it is not known) and its contents were gradually revealed in a
number of publications. In 1825, a biography of Captain Peter Heywood was
published in John Marshall's (editor) *Royal Naval Biography or, Memories of the
Services of all the Flag Officers, Superannuated Rear-Admirals, Retired Captains,
Post-Captains, and Commanders, Whose Names appeared on the Admiralty List of
Sea Officers at the commencement of the present year, or who have since been
promoted*, (1823-35). Heywood's entry contains detailed extracts from
Morrison's manuscripts and acknowledges their source. In 1831, Sir John
Barrow (Secretary to the Admiralty), using papers provided by Heywood,
was the anonymous author of *The Mutiny and Piratical Seizure of HMS
Bounty: its Cause and Consequences*, which included more extracts from
Morrison's manuscripts and gave them a wide circulation. Barrow's book,
since republished in numerous editions, is perhaps the fairest account of what
happened. In 1870, Lady Belcher, Peter Heywood's step-daughter, and the
estranged wife of Admiral Sir Edward Belcher (she had accused him of giving

her VD on her wedding night and of submitting her to other indignities) published *The Mutineers of the* Bounty *and their Descendants in Pitcairn and Norfolk Islands.* This included extracts from Morrison's *Journal,* then in her possession. Lady Belcher not only made Morrison's account of the mutiny and his views on who caused it, widely available in her own book (which was also published in the United States), she also lent Morrison's manuscript to William Fletcher, who used it to give a public lecture ('Fletcher Christian and the Mutineers of the *Bounty*', in *Transactions of the Cumberland Association for the Advancement of Literature and Science, Part II, 1876-77,* Carlisle) to an audience in Christian's home town of Cockermouth. Thus, within 80 years of Morrison writing his version of the affair, his views were well known to anybody interested in the *Bounty*.

It was not, however, until Owen Rutter edited a limited edition of Morrison's Journal in 1935 in the Golden Cockerel Press series (*The Journal of James Morrison, Boatswain's Mate of the* Bounty, *Describing the Mutiny & Subsequent Misfortunes of the Mutineers, Together with an Account, of the Island of Tahiti*) that Morrison's story was published in full.

While Morrison's manuscripts failed to become widely known until long after his death in 1807, and then largely due to the efforts of his friend, Peter Heywood between 1825 and 1831 (Heywood died in 1831), the substance of his version of events on *Bounty* was of immediate interest to Christian's family (who naturally sought information about the fate of their relative and what had caused him to mutiny). Peter Heywood's family were friends of Fletcher Christian's family, both sets living in the Isle of Man at the time of *Bounty*'s departure for Tahiti. Both families also shared the experience of suffering a sudden financial crisis. In Heywood's case, his father had lost a well-paid post just before Bligh was collecting his crew for the *Bounty* voyage. Bligh responded to requests from Heywood's family to take the young boy with him (Bligh's wife, Elizabeth Betham, also from the Isle of Man knew the Heywoods). Fletcher Christian's case was more severe and ultimately might provide the full explanation for his emotional outburst that fateful morning. His mother had lost her family's fortune largely through ill-advised investments and had been forced to leave Cockermouth for the Isle of Man to escape pestering creditors. She also had to terminate the costly education of two of her sons, Charles and Fletcher, and send them prematurely out into the world to earn their living. Charles went to sea as a surgeon with the East India Company (during which voyage he mutinied against the "tyranny" of his captain) and Fletcher, the youngest, was sent to sea first as a midshipman in the Royal Navy (he completed one voyage) and then as a "young gentleman" with Bligh in the merchant service. What degree of resentment Fletcher felt at the interruption to his career, and at his elder brother Edward (who had completed his expensive education before the crisis) we cannot but conjecture. In my view, his disenchantment with his future, and his realization of his unsuitability for life as a naval officer, played some part in his rash decision to mutiny over a row with his captain, instead of following Fryer's advice to suffer in silence on these occasions.

When Heywood was released after his royal pardon, he immediately contacted Fletcher's brother, Edward, who was a professor of law. Edward Christian was an intelligent man. He knew that there was no point in trying to exonerate his brother. Three men had hanged for participating in a mutiny led by his brother, who would have no defence if he was captured, whatever the behaviour of his captain. Unable to save his brother's life, he could, however, save his reputation. To do this he had to undo Bligh's. He did this, using a brilliant device. Christian invited individual *Bounty* men to meet him and be questioned. To demonstrate the truth of what he reported, without having to disclose what he left out, he arranged for at least one other gentleman, sometimes more than one, to be in attendance. These gentlemen were named by Christian, and an impressive list they make too. However, he was less than candid in explaining their relationships with him and his brother. Those whose relationships can be identified turn out to have close local, family, or political ties with Edward Christian. Their politics show them to be radicals, much impressed with the early phases of the French Revolution (full details are given in C.S. Wilkinson, *The Wake of the Bounty*, 1953, which is the best source for material on the alleged escape of Fletcher Christian from Pitcairn and his return to Cumberland). Edward Christian had not set up an independent tribunal; it was a legal snare for Bligh, but one into which he did not fall.

Christian's report of his conversations was published as an Appendix to the prosecution minutes of the court-martial of the mutineers taken down by Stephen Barney: *Minutes of the Proceedings of the Court-Martial held at Portsmouth August 12 [sic] 1792 on ten persons charged with mutiny on board His Majesty's Ship* Bounty, London, 1794. The text of Barney's minutes, its *Appendix* by Edward Christian and Bligh's reply were published in the Everyman's Library series in 1938, and reprinted in 1981, edited by George Mackaness, as: *A Book of the 'Bounty': William Bligh and others*.

It was the *Appendix* which caused the stir. In it are detailed pages of criticism of Bligh's style of command and of the opinions of the crew (not always named) regarding Fletcher Christian. John Fryer and William Purcell feature in it more often than anybody else who is named, and they made good witnesses. Fryer, as Master, the senior officer after Bligh, makes telling points about how Fletcher conducted himself the night before the mutiny. Five years after the event, the coconut incident has assumed a central role in the final collapse of Fletcher Christian into mutiny. Fryer and Purcell testify how badly Fletcher Christian took Bligh's accusations that the officers had colluded with the thieves of the ship's nuts. Interestingly, in the *Appendix* it is Fletcher who is the man singled out for Bligh's abuse and not Edward Young, as Fryer first reported in 1790. The extraordinary drama of Christian planning to jump overboard with some planks and swim 30 miles to the nearest island, Tofoa, becomes public for the first time; as do the events on Tubuai, where Christian first tried to make a settlement. This is portrayed in an exceedingly bland light when in fact it was a bloody mess from start to finish. Christian's party murdered several score of islanders, and abducted and raped various women (behaviour which repeated in the smaller community in Pitcairn cost Christian and the others their lives).

The *Appendix* contained a serious embarrassment for Heywood — its disclosure of midshipman George Stewart's role in suggesting to Christian that it was possible for him to seize the ship, rather than commit suicide by jumping over the side ("When you go, Christian, we are ripe for anything", p.71). Heywood's defence at his court-martial rested entirely on his claim that he and Stewart were kept below by the mutineers against their will, and that Bligh, unaware of this circumstance, had misunderstood their absence from his side. Now, if Stewart had in any way suggested to Christian anything at all that could be construed as an incitement to mutiny, then this made risible the notion of Heywood and Stewart as gallant loyalists. Years later, when Captain Beechey visited Pitcairn and interviewed John Adams, he too received this damning version of Stewart's role, and he wrote to Heywood in 1830 asking for his comments on the contradiction between Adam's story and Heywood's own in his 1825 biography. Heywood

Right

Richard Beechey. John Adams, 1825? SLNSW (No.65)

John Adams, who signed the Bounty's *muster as Alexander Smith but later reverted to his true name, became a leader of the mutineers on Pitcairn Island. He had many descendants from several Tahitian "wives", and lived on the Island until 1829.*

Far right

John Adams gave Captain Beechey a full account of the mutiny and the history of Pitcairn Island. This document, written by the ship's clerk on paper watermarked 1824, includes a verbal statement signed J. Adams. SLNSW (No. 66)

John Adams' Tombstone. Kindly lent by the National Maritime Museum, London (No.67)

The lead-covered wooden board which marked the grave of John Adams, the last surviving mutineer, who died on Pitcairn Island aged sixty-five on 5 March 1829. This headstone was replaced by a carved stone sent from England in the 1850s.

denied the claims of Adams (reported in Sir John Barrow's account). Yet the record shows that not only did Adams claim in 1825 this to be Stewart's true role, but so did the *Bounty* men interviewed by Edward Christian in 1792-4, and also James Morrison in his *Journal* of 1792-3. Morrison went further and claimed that Christian had also told ''Hayward'', which was clearly a reference to Heywood, as Christian was not talking to, let alone confiding in, Hayward at that moment (the two names were often misspelt in the manuscripts) of his intention to quit the ship. Apparently, Bligh was not the only *Bounty* man given to economizing with the truth.

Bligh, however, comes out very badly in the *Appendix*. Whatever follies Christian had committed, Bligh is shown to have been ultimately responsible for them because of his bullying of Christian. Far from the mutiny being the conspiracy that Bligh made it out to be, or of it being motivated by the lure of Tahiti, the mutiny is seen to be the result of one man breaking another's sense of duty through personal insults and provocations beyond the latter's capacity to endure. That this view says nothing about Christian's emotional state as a result of his personal reactions to his family circumstances, nor anything about whether it was reasonable for a man aspiring to be a first lieutenant in the Royal Navy to crack under his captain's pressure to lick him into shape, is of little comfort to Bligh's reputation. This particular man did crack under this particular captain's pressure, and as far as Edward Christian was concerned it explained, without necessarily justifying, what had happened.

On his return from the successful voyage of *Providence* and *Assistant*, which completed the breadfruit voyage interrupted by the mutiny on *Bounty*, Bligh was forced to reconsider his career prospects. Edward Christian had used much of the time between receiving Heywood's letter praising Fletcher and meeting other members of the *Bounty* and Bligh's return to lobby against Bligh (he contacted Sir Joseph Banks, for example). The court-martial had also led to the Admiralty reappraising Bligh's future as a commander (though, given the post-captain system, with everybody's progress dependent solely on the attrition rate of those above them, it is not surprising that others would encourage a removal of Bligh from the list, if that would make way for them, or for their protégés).

Bligh felt the cold on his return and set about to reply to the *Appendix*. This duly appeared in *An Answer to Certain Assertions contained in the Appendix to a Pamphlet . . .*, London, 1795 (also contained in the Everyman's Library edition of 1981). It was not a full and decisive reply to the *Appendix*. Bligh seemed to assume that all he needed to do was to produce other documents showing contradictions in the moral standards of some of his critics and to imply that Edward Christian, as the brother of a mutineer, was an unreliable witness of what persons unknown, or unidentified, asserted about their commander. Bligh was a career naval officer who saw his duty as carrying out his King's and the Admiralty's commissions and as such was not given to justifying himself to subordinates, disaffected or otherwise. The Admiralty wanted the breadfruit transplanted from Tahiti to Jamaica and it was his duty, and that of everybody on board *Bounty*, to comply with that request. Any man who failed to carry out his duty was, in Bligh's view, beyond the pale and not worthy of a hearing on any complaints he might have about his officers. Thus, while we can see why Bligh approached the task of his *Answer* in the way he did, we must conclude that he missed an opportunity of ensuring his reputation in posterity. Certainly, Edward Christian felt that he had won the contest, for he published *A Short Reply to Capt. William Bligh's Answer* (1795).

Bligh has had a number of biographers, of which two should be mentioned here as being head and shoulders above the rest. Owen Rutter has been mentioned several times in connection with making available key documents relating to the *Bounty* story in the 1930s. He also wrote a perceptive biography of Bligh in 1936: *Turbulent Journey: A Life of William Bligh, Vice-Admiral of the Blue*. Long out of print, Rutter's assessment of the issues involved in the mutiny remain close to the good order and discipline view: at stake is the issue of *duty*. In so far as men have difficult, even tyrannical, commanders, the good of the service and in the ultimate the defence of the realm depend on their unquestioning professional obedience. Legalistically, Rutter comes down on the side of Bligh as a commander and places Bligh's personality in the context of his "turbulent" career.

The Australian historian, Dr George Mackaness, published the first serious biography of Bligh in 1931 (two volumes): *The Life of Vice-Admiral William Bligh, RN, FRS*. A revised one-volume edition also appeared in 1951. Mackaness was undoubtedly the leading scholar on Bligh and the *Bounty* mutiny throughout his life. As an historian, Mackaness brought the skills of his profession to bear on what was, and remains a historical topic of wide public interest. Using the original materials available in the Mitchell Library, Sydney, and several collections held by Bligh's descendants, Mackaness put together the first scholarly biography of the man at the centre of the *Bounty* controversy. He quotes extensively from Morrison's manuscripts and the large Bligh and Banks correspondence that has survived. Since 1931, much more material has come to light; indeed, Mackaness was instrumental in making available new key documents, in particular, the important manuscripts of Lieutenant Francis Godolphin Bond (Bligh's relative and his first lieutenant on HMS *Providence*).

Like many other writers on Bligh (for example, Dr H.V. Evatt: *Rum Rebellion: a study of the overthrow of Governor Bligh by John Macarthur and the New South Wales Corps*) Mackaness was also caught up in historical debates about Bligh's role as a governor of New South Wales in 1808-10 and, incredibly, what it meant for modern Australians in the 1930s (there was a political controversy about the Governor's powers in New South Wales at the time), and this tended to colour his, and his critics', judgments about

THEATRE ROYAL, DRURY-LANE:

This present SATURDAY, April 20, 1816,

Their Majesties' Servants will perform (4th time) a new romantick operatick Ballet Spectacle, (Founded on the recent Discovery of a numerous Colony, formed by, and descended from, the Mutineers of the Bounty Frigate,) called

PITCAIRN'S ISLAND.

With new and selected Musick, new Scenery, Dresses & Embellishments.

The Action and Dances composed by, and produced under the Direction of, Mr. BYRNE.

The vocal and melo-dramatick Musick composed and compiled by Mr. M. CORRI.

The Overture and Musick of the Dances selected from *Pleyel, Kreutzer, Cherubini, Paer,* and other eminent Composers, by Mr BYRNE.

The Scenery by Mr. GREENWOOD & Assistants — The Dresses by Mr. BANKS & Miss SMITH.

The Machinry by Mr. LETHBRIDGE.—The Decorations by Mr. MORRIS.

Christian, *(Chief of the Colony)* Mr. CARR,

Otoo & Ereeeo, *(his Grandsons)* Mr. COVENEY, Mr. EBSWORTH;

Captain of the English Vessel, Mr. J. SMITH;

Midships, *(Nephew to the Captain)* Mr. BARNARD,

Pipes, *(Boatswain)* Mr. SMITH.

Sailors,—Messrs. Minton, Whilmshurst Ebsworth, Jones, Dibble, Clark, Cook; Odwell, Mead, Wilson, Evans, Warner, Buggins, Caulfield, Seymour.

Otaheina & Oberea, *(Sisters, and Grand-Daughters to Christian)*

Miss JOHNSON, Miss S. HALFORD.

Characters in the Ballet.—Mr. OSCAR BYRNE,

Monsieur DUPREE,

Miss SMITH,

Miss TREE, Miss SMYTHERS, Miss HART, Mrs. BRYAN, Miss VALLANCY

Misses Brock, Smith, C.Smith, O'Brien, Brown, C.Carr, Manning, Aylett.

Natives.—Mr. BARNES, Mr. SIMMONDS.

Messrs. Appleby, Mathews, G.Wells, Cooper, Holman, Hope, Brown, Bemetzrieder, Goodman, Gouriet, Vials, Jameson, Gussio, Goodwin, Wells.

Mesdms. A.Scott, C.Scott, Stubbs, Wells, Hobbs, Fairbrother, Tanner, L.Carr, Bates, M.Bates, Barrett, Cooke, M.Cooke, Viale, Caulfield, Ivers.

After which (19th time) a NEW FARCE, called

WHAT NEXT?

The Characters by

Mr. DOWTON, Mr. BARNARD, Mr. HARLEY,—(first time)

Mr. KENT, Mr. OXBERRY, Mr. KNIGHT, Mr. HUGHES,

Mrs. ORGER, Miss IVERS, Mrs. HARLOWE.

To which will be added (2d time these 20 years) the Musical Farce called

THE TWO MISERS.

Gripe, Mr KNIGHT, Hunks, Mr. GATTIE. Lively, Mr. T. COOKE,

Haly, Mr. SMITH, Mustapha, Mr J. SMITH, Osman, Mr. COOKE.

Harriet, Mrs. DICKONS, Jenny, Miss KELLY.

Books of the Songs to be had in the Theatre, Price Ten-pence.

Vivant Rex et Regina!— No Money to be returned.—Lowndes, Printer, St. Louis-Court, Drury-Lane.

The new operatick Ballet Spectacle, called PITCAIRN's ISLAND, Continuing to be received with unanimous Applause throughout, will be repeated every Evening except *Tuesday* next, when will be performed

Garrick's Jubilee Ode, in Honour of *Shakspeare.*

Miss *NASH,*

In Consequence of the enthusiastick Applause with which she was honoured in the Opera of LOVE IN A VILLAGE, and to comply with the very numerous Applications for a Repetition of it, will perform the Part of ROSETTA again on Wednesday, and will appear in the Opera of the HAUNTED TOWER, on Friday.

The musical Farce of the TWO MISERS, having been received on its revival with unbounded Applause, will be repeated *this Evening.*

On *Monday,* (3d time) the CASTLE SPECTRE. *Angela,* Miss MURRAY, (her third Appearance in that Character.) With (5th time) PITCAIRN's ISLAND.

On *Tuesday,* (first time this Season) Mrs. COWLEY's Comedy of the BELLE's STRATAGEM. After which will be performed, with appropriate Musick, GARRICK's Ode to SHAKSPEARE. With (20th time) the Farce of WHAT NEXT?

On *Wednesday,* the comick Opera of LOVE IN A VILLAGE.

With (6th time) PITCAIRN's ISLAND.

On *Thursday* the Comedy of a TRIP to SCARBOROUGH. With(7th time) PITCAIRN ISLAND

On *Friday,* the comick Opera of the HAUNTED TOWER. *Lord William,* Mr. T. COOKE,

Lady Elinor, Miss NASH, *Adela,* Mrs. DICKONS. With (8th time) PITCAIRN's ISLAND.

A new Tragedy, and a new melo-dramatick Afterpiece,

Are in Preparation and will shortly be produced.

Theatre Royal, Drury Lane. Playbill: Pitcairn's Island, Romantick Operatick Ballet Spectacle ... (1816) SLNSW (No.107)

Following the visit of two British frigates, Briton *and* Tagus *in 1814, the English public was tantalised by the reports of life on Pitcairn Island. Semi-fictitious plays and stories were written based on the life of John Adams, a "Prospero" like figure who had thrown off his evil ways to create the most god-fearing community on earth.*

Bligh as the commander of *Bounty* 1787-89. The issues in these disputes over Bligh's role as a colonial governor rumbled on well into the 1950s and unfortunately became very acrimonious and bitterly personal. A flavour of the debate can be gleaned from reading M.H. Ellis's biography: *John Macarthur* (1955), which takes a polar opposite view on the overthrow of Bligh to that of Evatt and Mackaness. Recently, the National Library of Australia published Bartrum's minutes of George Johnston's court-martial in 1811. Edited by John Ritchie, *A Charge of Mutiny: The Court-Martial of Lieutenant Colonel George Johnston for deposing Governor William Bligh in the Rebellion of 26 January 1808* (Canberra 1988), gives a clear account of what happened in the 1808 rebellion and why (and who — John Macarthur — was behind it all) by presenting verbatim the evidence of prosecution and defence.

Turning to the contemporary debate about the mutiny, it is necessary to consider the scholarly studies of Rolf Du Rietz of Uppsala in Sweden. Du Rietz has taken over from Mackaness as the leading scholar on Bligh and the *Bounty*, and, in a series of monographs and articles published since 1962, he has done a great deal of analytical work on the mutiny and the original manuscripts and contemporary accounts. His more important studies have been published in two series of papers (unfortunately, so far, in limited editions only). The first was *Studia Bountyana*, published in 1965 and 1966. They were occasioned by Madge Darby's *Who Caused the Mutiny on the 'Bounty'?* (Angus and Robertson, Sydney, 1965), which put forward a psychological explanation for the breakdown of the earlier good relationship that there had been between Bligh and Christian. Darby argued that Christian's mutiny was not explained by Bligh's intolerable conduct as a harsh disciplinarian but by some Freudian defect, even a frustrated or guilty homosexuality in Christian. She also argued that midshipman Edward Young was the decisive influence in the crucial moments of the mutiny. Apart from the reference to Young in Fryer's *Journal*, he is totally ignored in all other accounts, and Darby found his role more sinister on this score alone. (Certainly there is cause for grave suspicions about Young's role in the bloody massacres on Pitcairn, as there is for the last survivor, John Adams).

Du Rietz did not agree that the mutiny needed an explanation of this kind, and he launched a thorough, often ill-tempered, polemic (which is his style) against Darby's theses: *The Causes of the* Bounty *Mutiny: some comments on a book by Madge Darby* (Studia Bountyana, vol 1). The Du Rietz thesis on the mutiny, which he bases on his unrivalled knowledge of the historical evidence (he is a bibliophile), is that it is fully explained by Bligh's conduct; in short, Bligh drove Christian to mutiny. His most telling point is to compare the effect on Christian of Bligh's style of behaviour as commander of *Bounty*, with its effect on Lieutenant Bond on *Providence*. Bond was Bligh's step-sister's son and sailed on *Providence* in the same role as Christian sailed on *Bounty*. From an experimental viewpoint, what greater fortune could a historian have: two closely related events in which the object of the experiment is served by a change in the critical variable, the captain's subordinate, and observing the reaction of each to the same influence, Bligh's conduct?

Bond's reaction to his relative's style of command had been made public by George Mackaness in two small papers published 1953 and 1960 respectively (*Fresh Light on Bligh: being some unpublished correspondence of Captain William Bligh, RN., and Lieutenant Francis Godolphin Bond, RN. with Lieutenant Bond's manuscript notes made on the voyage of HMS "Providence," 1791-1795*, and ''Extracts from a log-book of HMS *'Providence'* kept by Lieut. Francis Godolphin Bond, RN . . .'', *Journal and Proceedings of the Royal Australian*

Historical Society, 1960.) In Du Rietz's view, Bond corroborates the evidence of Bligh's tyrannical behaviour given in Fryer's *Journal*, Morrison's *Memorandums* and *Journal*, Edward Christian's *Appendix* and Heywood's entry in Marshall's biographies. Bond's criticism of Bligh bears on his general behaviour: "imperious", "want of modesty", an "ungovernable temper", "envy and jealousy" and "unparalleled pride". Bligh exposed Bond's alleged deficiencies as a navigator in public, demanded he attend to his duty rather than compose a journal of the voyage, kept him on duty watch, demanded he be acquainted with every transaction on board, and that he check with him every order he was about to issue. The list of complaints is as extensive as it is repetitive: in short, Bond was driven hard by Bligh and he resented it. Unlike Christian, he did not mutiny. Du Rietz is convinced that this solves the so-called problem of the mutiny: Bligh caused it.

Darby was by no means convinced by Du Rietz and she replied in *Studia Bountyana 2: The Causes of the* Bounty *mutiny: a short reply to Mr Rolf Du Rietz's comments* (1966). She quotes Bligh's extremely good personal and professional relations with Lieutenant Portlock, captain of the *Assistant*, sister ship of *Providence* on the voyage, and a comment from Lieutenant George Tobin, third lieutenant of *Providence*: "For myself I feel I am indebted to [Bligh]. It was the first ship in which I ever served as an Officer — I joined full of apprehension — I soon thought that he was not dissatisfied with me — it gave me encouragement and on the whole we journeyed smoothly. Once or twice indeed I felt the unbridled licence of his power of speech — Yet never without soon receiving something like an emollient plaister to heal the wound." She also quotes from others to show that Bligh's foul language was by no means unusual among officers at the time (though it might still have shocked the unworldly Christian).

The second set of monographs written by Du Rietz consists of three volumes in his *Banksia* series. Again they are polemical, but as always Du Rietz also contributes important material from the historical records on the *Bounty* men. His *Thoughts on the Present State of Bligh Scholarship (Banksia 1)* set out an historian's methodology for coping with the issues raised by the *Bounty* mutiny and was extremely critical of my own approach in *Bligh* (1978). *Banksia 2: Fresh Light on John Fryer of the* 'Bounty', and *Banksia 3, Peter Heywood's Tahitian Vocabulary and the Narratives by James Morrison: some notes on their origin and history*, make significant contributions to the history of the manuscripts and views of these important witnesses to the mutiny, and show where a lot of *Bounty* authors have made wrong inferences from wrong facts in the past. It would be a fair summary of Du Rietz's work to say that he has demolished the image of Bligh as portrayed by himself in his two books and as developed by other authors since, without (only just) going over the top and condemning Bligh altogether out of sight. Compare this approach with Alexander McKee in his *The Truth About the Mutiny on the* Bounty (1961), in which he portrays Bligh as an unprincipled swindler and liar. Du Rietz's approach can be seen in Bengt Danielsson's *What Happened on the* Bounty (1962) (to which Du Rietz contributed a lot of the material), while Danielsson added a lot of information about Tahitian society at the time of Bligh's visits.

Where does the historical record leave Bligh and the men of the *Bounty*? In one sense, not very much closer to the truth than was known (or accepted) in the years immediately after the mutiny. We know how some of the men involved saw the event and how they rated the principal figures involved. While Christian has left nothing in writing for historians to argue over, his views on what happened have been reported in detail by Morrison.

Fryer's assessment of what happened is also available. None of the men whose views have so far been discovered has any doubts about who caused the mutiny: universally they blame Bligh. Their assessments, of course, have nothing in common with the imaginative presentations of scriptwriters and film makers.

Bounty was not a happy ship, but not because of a physical tyranny by a stereotyped 18th century commanding officer — Bligh was never a flogger in any sense that would enrage an 18th century ship's crew. Nor did Bligh overstep the norm as a nagging officer. The Royal Navy had far worse martinets than Bligh, and many more who did not have any of his redeeming features. But Bligh did overstep the mark with Fletcher Christian — it was not Bligh crushing, so much as Christian crumbling, that brought things to a head. More than one seaman has deserted, even committed suicide, sometimes simply by disappearing over the side, because he could not take the petty bullying or constant mockery of a shipmate. Men in close confinement on long voyages were faced with intense psychological stresses hardly understood today, let alone in the 18th century (the incidence of sea-borne insanity was put down to the men banging their heads on the low beams). That Christian was highly stressed (Morrison thought him insane on one occasion) is beyond historical doubt. That he contemplated jumping overboard and becoming a statistic — ''man lost at sea'' — is also beyond doubt (in which case hardly anybody would have heard of HMS *Bounty*). But he did not go through with his plan (as, perhaps, many other young men facing similar stresses decide as their fury cools). Instead, he set about arranging his seizure of the ship. The rest, as they say, is history, but none the less mysterious and riveting for that.

Gavin Kennedy is the author of "Bligh" (1978), "The Death of Captain Cook" (Duckworth, 1978) and "Captain Bligh: the man and his mutinies" (Duckworth, 1989, Cardinal, 1990.)

ARRESTING BLIGH

Paul Brunton

The foolhardy rebellion against Bligh in New South Wales presents a mirror-image of the bungling mutiny on HMS *Bounty*. Both took place in settings stripped of the hallmarks of British imperial authority: one in a bare continent, the other in the middle of the Pacific Ocean.

The instigators, Fletcher Christian and John Macarthur, had identified closely with a world Bligh had entered briefly. Christian wished to remain in the exotic paradise of the Pacific; Macarthur wished to remain in the colony and preside over an independent empire.

Both instigators were unstable. Before the mutiny Christian had contemplated suicide and he ended his days in bloody conflict with his fellow mutineers. Macarthur died a certified lunatic after a career of aggression, antagonism and conflict.

After surviving two rebellions and the attendant rancour, Bligh was promoted to Vice-Admiral of the Blue and retired peacefully to a country house in Kent with his daughters.

Bligh assumed office in New South Wales on 13 August 1806 and was deposed, and placed under arrest by Major George Johnston, commander of the New South Wales Corps at Sydney, on Tuesday 26 January 1808 — the twentieth anniversary of the foundation of the colony.

Bligh was removed because he was a tyrant and the people were about to rebel against him, plunging the colony into chaos. This, at least, was the justification of those who committed the act of treason.

Philip Gidley King, Bligh's predecessor, had governed since 28 September 1800 during which time he had taken measures to limit the trading monopoly of the officers of the New South Wales Corps, the military detachment assigned to the colony, and to stop the use, as a currency, of rum, a generic name for all spirits.

He had sent John Macarthur, a captain in the Corps, to England in November 1801 for court-martial resulting from a duel he had fought with his commanding officer, Lieutenant-Colonel William Paterson in which the latter had been wounded.

King left his superiors in London in no doubt of his view of Macarthur. He wrote on 8 November 1801:

> His employment during the eleven years he has been here has been that of making a large fortune, helping his brother officers to make small ones (mostly at the publick expence) and sowing discord and strife . . . Experience has convinced every man in this colony that there are no resources which art, cunning, impudence, and a pair of basilisk eyes can afford that he does not put in practice to obtain any point he undertakes . . . If the records of this colony,

now in your office, are examined you will find his name very conspicuous. Many and many instances of his diabolical spirit had shown itself before Gov'r Phillip left this colony, and since, altho' in many instances he has been the master worker of the puppetts he has set in motion . . . And should any further proofs be wanting of the restless and turbulent conduct of Capt'n Jno. McArthur . . . I must require that the evidence of the late Governors Philip and Hunter may be procured, which, with many documents now in the Secretary of State's office, will fully prove that this conduct of Capt'n McArthur's has not been confined to the present moment.[1]

In 1789, John Macarthur, not yet 22, had transferred to the New South Wales Corps, then being raised in England, with the express purpose of improving his financial position. He arrived in Sydney in 1790. His charismatic personality quickly established him as a leader and during the 33 months from Phillip's departure in December 1792 to the arrival of Hunter in September 1795 he benefitted greatly from the military governments of Grose and Paterson through land grants, monopoly trading and his positions as regimental paymaster and Inspector of Public Works.

When he was despatched to London by King, he took the opportunity of taking some examples of wool from his estate at Elizabeth Farm, Parramatta. He sailed, fortuitously as it transpired, via the Moluccas, where at Amboina he formed a friendship with Sir Robert Farquhar, whose father was physician to the Prince of Wales and was related to Lord Camden. In 1804 Camden would take over as Secretary of State for War and the Colonies. It was also fortuitous that at this time British manufacturers were seeking new sources of wool, Napoleon's campaigns having threatened the reliability of the traditional source, Spain.

The army's advocate-general found it impossible to decide Macarthur's case at such a distance. It was thought King should have handled the dispute locally and although both parties were criticized it was made clear to King that no further action should be taken against Macarthur.

Macarthur resigned from the army and on the basis of his wool samples and his persuasiveness obtained Camden's permission to spearhead the development of a wool industry in New South Wales. Having left the colony in 1801 to be court-martialled at the Governor's insistence, he returned in June 1805 in possession of sheep from the Royal flocks and with instructions to King to grant him "not less than" 5,000 acres. The Governor had been well and truly vanquished.

Macarthur wished his grant to be at the Cowpastures — the best grazing land which had to that date been discovered. The instruction which Camden sent to King did not specify the location of the grant. This enabled King to prevaricate, to grant Macarthur the Cowpastures land provisionally and to refer to London for clarification — a process which could take over a year.

King had written in a private letter to the Home Office in June 1802 that if Macarthur were allowed to return to New South Wales and join the other "turbulent characters" in the Corps then:

> my recall, or permission to return, will be absolutely necessary, to prevent such steps being taken by me as will not much tend to the quiet and good of the colony; for to serve under such a set as will then be in the colony, is what neither my pride will stoop to, nor situation allow of.[2]

By May 1803, even before Macarthur's return, King was telling Lord Hobart that in discharging his duty as Governor he was attracting the "assassinating and dark attacks of those who dare not avow themselves" as well as "opposition and insults" from those "who ought to have shewn a different

line of conduct" and he made it quite clear that he was referring to the officers of the New South Wales Corps.[3]

He asked Hobart to appoint a commission to examine the state of the colony and, if this were not possible, to grant him leave of absence in order that he could put his case direct in London. King was granted neither request and in June 1804 received a reply which indicated that he would be replaced as governor.

Macarthur had not charmed everyone in London. Sir Joseph Banks was not convinced of the soundness of Macarthur's proposals. Banks had played a major role in the development of New South Wales since he had himself been to Botany Bay with James Cook in 1770 and, in his journal, produced the first extended account of the Australian continent. He was the confidant of Governors Phillip, Hunter and King and had enjoyed considerable influence with British ministers on the administration of the colony.

Banks did not favour a large land grant to one person but thought the wool industry should be developed by an English company. Macarthur could, if he wished, be the local manager. Banks believed that Macarthur had over-estimated the quality of the grazing land available.

Banks was well aware of Macarthur's reputation for fractiousness in the colony. Whether he actually had Macarthur's grant reduced from 10,000 to 5,000 acres is unclear but Macarthur certainly thought so.

It was reported to Banks that Macarthur had boasted how he had insulted the former in August 1804 at the sale of sheep from the Royal flocks and, when back in New South Wales, spoke of Sir Joseph as as "venal & debauched an old rascall" as any of His Majesty's ministers.[4] The language is typical of Macarthur. It indicates a level of frustration at Banks' ability to interfere with his plans. A similar tone would be employed when later speaking about Bligh.

Banks continued to be wary of Macarthur. In a paper which he submitted to the Board of Trade in August 1806, he presented a case against granting further "indulgencies" to Macarthur. These included the argument that if Macarthur were rewarded other wool growers would want similar treatment, Banks' belief that Macarthur had no practical farming knowledge and "his General character which is that of having made a Large sum of money in N.S.W. by Trafficing with the new settlers & exchanging the Stock etc given them by Government for Liquor". This "gives no hopes of his being a good subject in Fact his visit to England as he modestly terms it was under an arrest."[5]

Macarthur was in New South Wales and Banks was in England. Soon, however, Banks' protege would be in New South Wales confronting Macarthur direct.

Though King had received the news of his recall in mid-1804 it was not until August 1806 that he was replaced by William Bligh. Bligh's appointment was orchestrated by Banks.

In March 1805 Banks was consulted by the Government about a suitable replacement for King. On the 15th of that month he wrote to Bligh requesting him to consider the post. Banks listed the following qualities required in the person who took up this appointment:

> one who had integrity unimpeached, a mind capable of providing its own resources in difficulties without leaning on others for advice, firm in discipline, civil in deportment and not subject to whimper and whine when severity of discipline is wanted to meet emergencies.[6]

An independent man not afraid to discipline others was required.

Banks offered several inducements to attract a senior naval officer living on

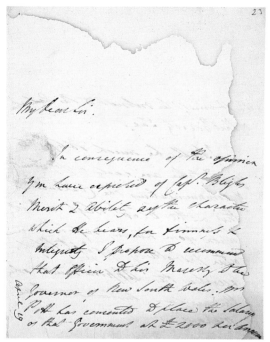

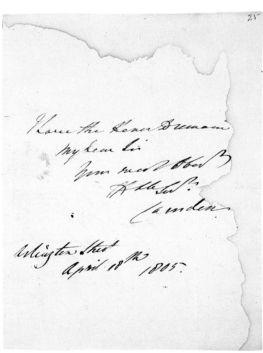

'In consequence of the opinion you have expressed of Capt. Bligh's merit & ability & of the character which he bears, for firmness & Integrity I propose to recommend that officer to his Majesty to be Governor of New South Wales.'
Letter from Lord Camden to Sir Joseph Banks agreeing to appoint William Bligh Governor of New South Wales.
SLNSW (No. 82)

his naval salary with several unmarried daughters to support: double the salary of his predecessor, "the whole of the Government power and stores at your disposal", his naval rank to continue allowing him to be eligible for future promotion, and better marriage prospects for his daughters. Banks was not this time simply using his influence to help Bligh; he was actually exerting pressure on Bligh to accept the post.

Banks wanted a man who would confront the New South Wales Corps and Macarthur. Banks was not ignorant of Bligh's reputation as a disciplinarian: he chose him for that reason. The *Warrior* incident would have been fresh in his memory.

Bligh had been court-martialled earlier in 1805 over an incident on his ship *Warrior*. Bligh was reprimanded and "admonished to be in future more correct in his language". In his own defence, Bligh had given a character assessment which showed considerable self-knowledge:

> I candidly and without reserve avow that I am not a tame & indifferent observer of the manner in which Officers placed under my orders conducted themselves in the performance of their several duties; a signal or any communication from a commanding officer have ever been to me an indication for exertion & alacrity to carry into effect the purport thereof & peradventure I may occasionally have appeared to some of those officers as unnecessarily anxious for its execution by exhibiting any action or gesture peculiar to myself to such: Gentlemen, [I now] appeal to you, Mr President & the members of this honourable Court, who know & have experienced the arduous task of responsibility and that of the magnitude of one of his Majesty's seventy-four gun ships, which will, I am persuaded acquit me of any apparent impetuosity & would plead in extenuation for my imputed charges: attributing the warmth of temper, which I may at intervals have discovered, to my zeal for that service in which I have been employed without an imaginary blemish on my character for upwards of thirty five years and not with a premeditated view of any personal insult to my Prosecutor . . .[7]

And just one week before Banks asked Bligh to accept the Governorship, Bligh had written to him:

> I have been bred up in such a state of watchfulness & care and under such a high sense of professional duty that perhaps I may be too particular in the execution of it.[8]

On 22 April 1805, King George approved the choice of Bligh as Governor. Bligh sailed for Port Jackson in February 1806 and arrived in August. He was 52 years old. His wife, Elizabeth, was too ill to accompany him and he took his daughter, Mary, and her husband, Lieutenant John Putland, the latter to act as his aide-de-camp.

Even before he landed at Sydney Cove on 6 August the stage was set for the drama that would engulf him 18 months later. The new Governor had a past — "Bounty Bligh" as he was known in some circles — which some liked to imagine proved beyond doubt that he was a tyrant. He was coming to administer a colony which had not accepted Vice-Regal direction since the officers of the New South Wales Corps had held absolute power from December 1792 to September 1795. Macarthur was a central character in, and a leading beneficiary of, this interregnum.

Neither Hunter nor his successor King had been able to govern effectively in the face of such opposition. Bligh was the protege of Sir Joseph Banks, a man whom Macarthur saw as a threat to his plans to become the squire of the Cowpastures.

The new governor was a disciplinarian. He was absolutely immovable when he believed he was right, which was most of the time, a trait he shared with Macarthur. He had a history of using strong language, though he was never physically violent. He would follow his instructions to the letter regardless of local circumstances. The situation was inflammatory from the beginning.

On Bligh's first day he was presented with an address of welcome signed by George Johnston, on behalf of the military; Richard Atkins, on behalf of the civil authorities; and John Macarthur, on behalf of the free inhabitants. It was ironic that these three men would be intimately connected with his

Artist unknown. Miniature portrait of Mary Putland (nee Bligh), c.1800. SLNSW (No.85)

Bligh's daughter Mary was the only member of his family to accompany him to New South Wales. She was an attractive woman and a social success in the colony despite her taste in dress which shocked the more conservative colonists. Her first husband died in 1807 and at 27 she remarried Lieutenant-Governor Maurice O'Connell, second-in-charge to Bligh's successor, Governor Macquarie. Mary O'Connell came back to New South Wales for 10 years from 1838-1848 and died in London in 1864.

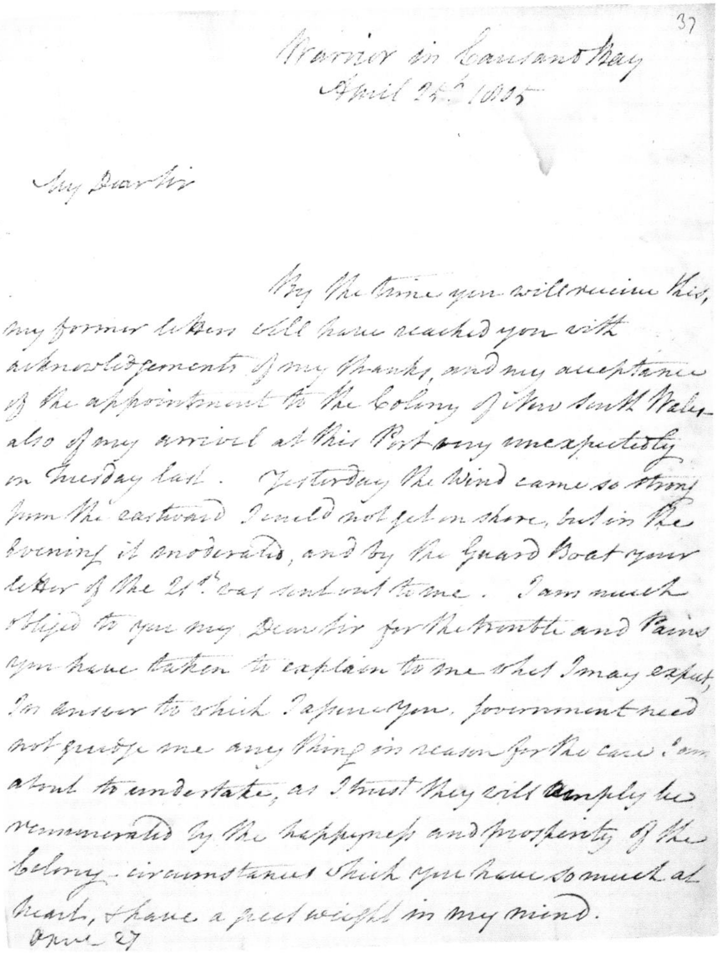

37

Warrior in Cawsand Bay
April 24th 1805

My Dear Sir

By the time you will receive this, my former letters will have reached you with acknowledgements of my thanks, and my acceptance of the appointment to the Colony of New South Wales also of my arrival at this Port very unexpectedly on Tuesday last. Yesterday the Wind came so strong from the eastward I could not get on shore, but in the Evening it moderated, and by the Guard Boat your letter of the 21st was sent out to me. I am much obliged to you my Dear Sir for the trouble and Pains you have taken to explain to me what I may expect, In answer to which I assure you, Government need not grudge me any thing in reason for the care I am about to undertake, as I trust they will amply be remunerated by the happiness and prosperity of the Colony. circumstances which you have so much at heart, & have a great weight in my mind.

Over 27

In this letter written from HMS Warrior *at Cawsand Bay, Plymouth, Bligh thanks his sponsor, Sir Joseph Banks, and accepts the appointment to the post of Governor of New South Wales.*

'By the time you will receive this, my former letters will have reached you with acknowledgment of my thanks, and my acceptance of the appointment to the Colony of New South Wales also of my arrival at this Port very unexpectedly on Tuesday last.'
SLNSW (No. 83)

deposition: Atkins, who would be the catalyst; Johnston, who took the decisive step; and Macarthur who engineered it.

Even an action as seemingly innocent as this caused dissension. A group of 379 free settlers presented a separate petition on Bligh claiming that Macarthur could not speak on their behalf:

> we beg to observe that had we deputed anyone,John McArthur would not have been chosen by us, we considering him an unfit person to step forward upon such an occasion, as we may chiefly attribute the rise in the price of mutton to his withholding the large flock of wethers he now has to make such price as he may choose to demand.[9]

This only confirmed what Bligh would have been told about Macarthur by Banks.

It would be only a matter of weeks before the first clash between Macarthur, now aged 39, and Bligh would occur and it was over the former's plans for the wool industry. At the court-martial of George Johnston in 1811 Macarthur was asked "Did Gov. Bligh promote the intentions of Government in your favour, and forward your agricultural views?" Macarthur answered "Never, in the smallest degree". Macarthur then outlined an interview he had with Bligh at Government House, Parramatta, "about a month after he had taken the command." Macarthur mentioned his plans for the wool industry and his grant of 5,000 acres which King would not confirm. According to Macarthur, Bligh:

George William Evans (attrib.) Government House, Parramatta 1808-1809? SLNSW (No.81)

This site was used as a vice-regal residence until 1857. The house occupied by Bligh was a two storey building erected by Governor Hunter in 1799. The core of the old house exists today inside the later renovations.

Artist unknown. Government Agricultural Establishment, Castle Hill, 1806? SLNSW (No.81)

Bligh was interested in establishing a sound agricultural economy with farms for settlers and ex-convicts. He did not approve of the monopoly in rum trading run by officers of the New South Wales Corps.

burst out instantly into a most violent passion, exclaiming, 'What have I to do with your sheep, sir; what have I to do with your cattle? Are you to have such flocks of sheep and such herds of cattle as no man ever heard of before? — No, sir! . . . I have heard of your concerns, sir; you have got 5,000 acres of land in the finest situation in the country; but by God, you shan't keep it!'[10]

Macarthur then allegedly told Bligh that he had received his grant at the recommendation of the Privy Council and by order of the Secretary of State. This, according to Macarthur, led to the following outburst by Bligh: "Damn the Privy Council! and damn the Secretary of State, too!"[11]

The accuracy of the words alleged by Macarthur, remembered almost five years after the event, is irrelevant. Clearly, Macarthur from the beginning of

Bligh's rule saw him as the great obstacle to the realization of his ambitions.

Early in February 1807, Bligh wrote to William Windham, Secretary of State for War and the Colonies, attempting to have Macarthur's grant relocated. Windham's successor, Viscount Castlereagh, did not answer this until December 1807 and by the time this was received in the colony, Bligh had been deposed. Throughout 1807 Macarthur would have been in an anxious state over the land grant — the jewel of his empire.

Bligh set about reforming the colony. In October 1806, new port regulations were issued; in January 1807 it was made mandatory for all promissory notes to be payable only in sterling; the next month King's order against illicit stills was re-issued and the use of liquor for barter was forbidden.

All sensible and necessary measures but like all political reforms not welcomed by those who would be affected to their disadvantage. Bligh's claim that town leases were invalid and his demolition of some houses on such leases was, even if justified on legal and social grounds, confrontational and angered those in the New South Wales Corps who were affected or likely to be. Further, Bligh's insistence that even those with letters from the Under-Secretary of State recommending land grants needed formal approval from London was unnecessarily obstructive though it was legally correct. This was especially inflammatory when the same criterion was not applied to the three extensive grants bestowed on Bligh by King and the subsequent land grant by Bligh to Mrs King. Bligh's own farm on the Hawkesbury was never affected by the shortage of convicts, an action which in its insensitivity could only provoke hostility.

George William Evans (attrib.) Government House, Sydney, 1808-1809? SLNSW (No.81) First Government House, Sydney stood on the south-western corner of Bridge and Phillip Streets. It was replaced by the present Government House in 1845. Bligh was arrested in Government House on the evening of 26 January 1808, in the Rum Rebellion takeover.

However, having said this, it must be noted that the complaints about Bligh prior to his arrest rarely mention specific grievances or, at least, these are submerged in rhetoric about the loss of liberty and the new age of tyranny.

As early as January 1807, Elizabeth Macarthur was writing to her friend at home, Miss Kingdon:

> The Governor has already shown the inhabitants of Sydney that he is violent — rash — tyrannical. No very pleasing prospect at the beginning of his reign.[12]

These sentiments expressed less than six months into his governorship were no doubt absorbed from her husband and his associates.

In 1790, when Bligh had returned to England following the mutiny on HMS *Bounty* he had been a hero. He had survived an epic voyage of 5,822 kilometres in a tiny boat with little food. The Christian family was silent at the ignominious end of a promising son.

While Bligh was on his second breadfruit voyage on HMS *Providence*, from 1791 to 1793, some of the mutineers were captured at Tahiti and placed on trial in September 1792. Bligh being out of the country could not defend himself.

As a result of the campaigns launched by Christian's brother and others to justify the actions of the mutineers a view emerged which attributed the mutiny to Bligh's tyranny. While this was unjustified, by the time Bligh returned the view had become entrenched in some quarters. In New South Wales, those who wished to be rid of him realized that his reputation made him vulnerable.

Macarthur was opposed to all governors as Hunter and King could testify. He had a particular reason to oppose Bligh, the nominee of Banks. In alleging tyranny, Macarthur would show that Bligh was running true to form. But it is conceivable that as time went on Macarthur believed his own propaganda. It would not be difficult for Macarthur to see Bligh as illiberal and tyrannical because he opposed those plans of Macarthur's which he believed to be right.

Other letters of a later date employ the same language as Elizabeth Macarthur. John Blaxland wrote:

> The Governor is behaving so very arbitrary that I do not consider either my person or property safe a single hour . . . every species of injustice and oppression is exercised in its full force.[13]

Lieutenant William Minchin commented:

> . . . a deluge worse than that of the Hawkesbury has since swept off every path to . . . industry and happiness . . . if a Military Officer might be allowed to use the words Tyranny and oppression, I would inform you that until now I never experienced their weight.[14]

John Harris reported:

> . . . it is completely the reign of Robertspere [sic], or that of Terror . . . I have heard much said of Bounty Bligh before I saw him, but no person could conceive that he could be such a fellow . . . Caligula himself never reigned with more despotic sway than he does.[15]

And Elizabeth Macarthur on 21 October 1807 returned to her theme:

> Food, clothing and every necessary of life bear a price truly astonishing. All these melancholy changes may be considered the effect of tyranny and an improper administration of the law. Liberty has retired from amongst us into the pathless wilds.[16]

The military certainly had some complaints against Bligh though it is unclear how widespread or significant they were. The measures to stop the barter in liquor were never successful. The dispute over the town leases affected only a few soldiers. Bligh did choose officers for court duty without consulting the commanding officer but how much this upset the rank-and-file is unknown.

Johnston did send a complaint to Sir James Gordon, the secretary to the Duke of York, Commander-in-Chief of the British army in October 1807. However, as with the other documents, the language was chosen to re-inforce the popular view of Bligh. Johnston wrote of the:

> glaring acts of Governor Bligh's indecorous and, I hope I might be pardoned to say, oppressive conduct . . . Governor Bligh seems ignorant of any instructions or rules whatever, but such as are dictated by the Violent passion of the moment.[17]

In the same month, the following verse with its direct reference to the mutiny on HMS *Bounty* was circulating in Sydney.

> Oh tempora! Oh Mores! Is there
> no Christian in New South Wales to put
> a stop to the Tyranny of the Governor.[18]

In this atmosphere, any incident which could be interpreted as an excessive use of power on Bligh's behalf could provide the catalyst for action against him. Those who attempted this could use as their justification Bligh's reputation for tyrannical rule which they themselves had been nurturing.

In December 1807, the Judge-Advocate, the alcoholic Richard Atkins, issued a warrant to the chief constable at Parramatta, Francis Oakes, summoning Macarthur to appear before the Bench of Magistrates at 10am on 16 December for a breach of the landing regulations. This arose over Macarthur's refusal to pay or victual the crew of his ship *Parramatta* forcing them to come on shore when the ship had been placed under arrest.

Macarthur had refused to pay a bond of £900 which he had forfeited because a convict had escaped on the *Parramatta* on its recent voyage to Tahiti. All shipowners forfeited such a bond if any convict escaped on their ships. The incident is complicated but the salient fact is that rather than pay £900 Macarthur preferred to abandon a ship valued at £10,000 in order to engineer a dispute with Atkins and ultimately with the Governor.

Oakes went to Elizabeth Farm late in the evening of 15 December in order to deliver the warrant. Macarthur handed Oakes a note which stated:

> Mr Oakes, —
>   You will inform the persons who sent you here with the warrant you have now shewn me, . . . that I never will submit to the horrid tyranny that is attempted until I am forced; that I consider it with scorn and contempt, as I do the persons who have directed it to be executed.[19]

This was rebellion — a deliberate assault on the authority of the Judge-Advocate and the Governor.

The next morning Macarthur was arrested at the home of Charles Grimes, the Surveyor-General, four doors away from Government House in Bridge Street. Macarthur had come from Parramatta knowing he would be arrested and no doubt wishing, for dramatic effect, to do this in a public place. He was granted bail until the next day when he was committed for trial before the Criminal Court on 25 January 1808. He remained on bail. This gave him

John William Lewin.
Sydney Cove, 1808.
SLNSW
(No.81)

A view of Sydney in
William Bligh's time.
Lewin, Australia's first
professional artist, was one
of the small landholders in
the Hawkesbury district who
remained loyal to Bligh
after the Rebellion.

over one month to plan, to fulminate about tyranny and to use his influence
with the Corps to gain its support.

On the morning of 25 January the court assembled. It consisted of the
Judge-Advocate and six officers of the Corps: Anthony Fenn Kemp, John
Brabyn, William Moore, Thomas Laycock, William Minchin and William
Lawson.

Before Atkins was sworn, Macarthur protested against his sitting on the
court. He had a number of grounds and read from a lengthy document and
towards the conclusion declaimed the following:

> You will now decide, gentlemen, whether law and justice shall finally prevail
> . . . You have the eyes of an anxious public upon you, trembling for the
> safety of their property, their liberty, and their lives. To you has fallen the lot
> of deciding a point which perhaps involves the happiness or misery of millions
> yet unborn. I conjure you in the name of Almighty God, in whose presence
> you stand, to consider the inestimable value of the precious deposit with which
> you are now entrusted.[20]

He then gave the Corps its rallying call:

> It is to the officers of the New South Wales Corps that the administration of
> Justice is committed; and who that is just has anything to dread?[21]

The sequence of events driving the colony into a state of rebellion took place
within 33 hours and would culminate ironically on Australia Day.

Atkins threatens to gaol Macarthur. Kemp retaliates by threatening to gaol
Atkins who then leaves for Government House, declaring that there is no
court without him. Atkins leaves behind his papers, which detail the charges
against Macarthur.

At 11.15am the six officers in their court room at the lower end of Bridge
Street send a note to Bligh at Government House further up the hill. It
requests him to replace Atkins as Judge-Advocate. At 12.30pm Bligh replies
that there is no cause to challenge Atkins and that he, Bligh, has no power
to remove the Judge-Advocate from office and that without the latter there is
no legally constituted court.

About 1pm the officers reply stating that they will not serve with Atkins
in a trial of Macarthur. At 2.15pm Bligh demands that Atkins' papers and
the paper that Macarthur read to the court be sent to him. The officers
refuse and at 3.30pm they inform Bligh that Macarthur has asked for military
protection because he is in fear of his life — a theatrical move on
Macarthur's part to heighten the tension.

At 3.45pm Bligh again demands the papers and re-iterates that without Atkins there is no court. At 5.00pm copies of the papers are sent to Bligh but the originals remain with the officers and Bligh is informed that the "court" has adjourned. Macarthur has been "remanded to his former bail"

At 5.30pm Bligh writes to the Corps' commanding officer at Sydney, George Johnston, who lives at Annandale, asking him to come to Government House. Johnston sends a message to say he is too ill. He had in fact fallen from his carriage, drunk, after the mess dinner on the previous evening.

At 9am on Tuesday 26 January Macarthur is again arrested at Bligh's command and taken to the gaol. At 10am the six officers re-assemble. They write again to Bligh requesting a new Judge-Advocate and the release of Macarthur on bail. This communication is ignored.

In the afternoon Bligh sends a note to the officers summoning them to Government House at 9am the following morning indicating that Atkins has charged them with "certain crimes". Bligh informs Johnston of his action and tells him that the actions of his officers are considered treasonable. Johnston now hurries to town, not to Government House but to the barracks.

At his court-martial Johnston described the events of that afternoon:

> On my arrival, as I passed through the streets, everything denoted terror and consternation: I saw in every direction groups of people with soldiers amongst them, apparently in deep and earnest conversation. I repaired immediately to the barrack; and, in order to separate the military from the people, made the drum beat the orders.[22]

Johnston claimed that at the barracks "an immense number of the people, comprising all the respectable inhabitants, except those who were immediately

'To Major Geo. Johnston Lieut Governor & — Comman[d]ing the N.S.Wales Corps — Sir,
    The present alarming state of this colony; in which every man's property liberty and Life is endangered induces us most earnestly to implore you instantly to place Governor Bligh under an arrest and to assume the command of the Colony. — We pledge ourselves at a moment of less agitation to come foreward to support the measure with our fortunes and our lives —'
John Macarthur drafted this letter, calling on Major George Johnston to arrest Governor Bligh. The letter was signed by over 150 people. Most signatures were obtained after Bligh's arrest. SLNSW (No. 97)

Artist unknown. Arrest of Governor Bligh, 1808. SLNSW (No.96)

Painted at the time of the Rebellion, as anti-Bligh propaganda. The drawing shows a cowardly Bligh being dragged from under a bed in the servant's room of Government House at the time of his arrest by Lieutenant William Minchin of the New South Wales Corps. The court-martial of George Johnston who assumed command of the colony after the rebellion established that this picture was libellous as the space under the bed was narrow and Bligh rather stout.

connected with Capt. Bligh''[23] begged him to arrest Bligh if only to protect him, otherwise an insurrection and massacre would occur. Johnston did not act immediately. He first ordered Macarthur to be released from gaol, an action for which he had no authority. When the latter arrived he suggested that Johnston should not arrest Bligh without a written petition. Johnston said at his court martial: "He (ie Macarthur) drew up a paper to that effect, which as soon as laid on the table was filled with as many signatures as it could contain".[24] This is not true. A few signatures were inscribed at the time, perhaps five. The rest were added after the rebellion.

Macarthur in this document continued the use of that language that he had been using now for over a year. He referred to "every man's property, liberty, and life" being in danger.

At sun-down, the New South Wales Corps, about 400 in number, in full battle formation and with their arms in readiness, marched the short distance from the barracks in George Street up Bridge Street to Government House. Johnston led with his hand in a sling and the band played the "British Grenadiers.".

It took some time to find Bligh, up to two hours according to one account. He was in a tiny steward's room on the first floor busy destroying papers or secreting them on his person. He had dressed in full naval uniform. It may have taken such a time to find him because, on Bligh's account, he was discovered earlier by Lieutenant Moore who kept this information ·from his comrades. Not all soldiers viewed with equanimity the deposition of a governor.

It was alleged Bligh was found hiding under or behind a bed. This may have been true but it was not because of cowardice. He saw no reason to submit to illegitimate authority.

Bligh was arrested and confined to Government House. Johnston declared martial law and assumed the position of Lieutenant-Governor. The next day he issued a proclamation which stated in part:

> In future no man shall have just cause to complain of violence, injustice, or oppression. No free man shall be taken, imprisoned, or deprived of his house, land, or liberty, but by the law. Justice shall be impartially administered, without regard to, or respect of persons; and every man shall enjoy the fruits of his industry and security.[25]

The language, as Bligh himself observed, was reminiscent of the rhetoric of the French revolution.

Bligh's arrest had been planned between 17 December 1807 when Macarthur was committed for trial and his trial on 25 January 1808. Although we know nothing of what plans were made nor how detailed they were it is obvious that Macarthur was the ringleader. It was he who, crying tyranny, had defied the warrant for his arrest and he who, having challenged Atkins, read a prepared speech reminding the large audience of the threat to liberty, property and life. Johnston ensured that Macarthur was released from gaol before any move against Bligh was made. He needed Macarthur's counsel.

Bligh was confined at Government House for one year. He resolutely refused to sail to England until he was relieved by lawful authority. In January 1809 he was ordered to relinquish command of his ship HMS *Porpoise* on which he had arrived in the colony. He refused to comply and was placed under guard in the barracks for one week. It was proposed that he should return to England in the *Porpoise*. He agreed and, once in control of the ship, reneged. As he said at Johnston's court-martial:

Robert Dighton. Lt. Colonel
George Johnston, 1810.
SLNSW
(No.88)
Taken from a watercolour
done in London in 1810 at
the time of his court-martial,
this portrait shows Johnston
in the uniform of the New
South Wales Corps.
Johnston took control of the
colony from 26 January to
28 July 1808.

'An Account of The
Rebellion' sent by William
Bligh to Sir Joseph Banks.
SLNSW (No. 99)

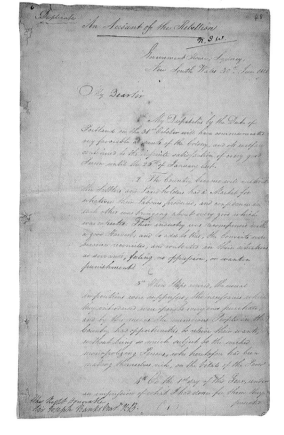

'The Tyrant is now no
doubt gnashing his teeth
with vexation at his
overthrow — may he often
have cause to do the like!'
Letter from John Macarthur
to his wife Elizabeth,
describing the arrest of
Governor Bligh, 1808.
SLNSW (No. 94)

> I do hereby Certify, that when I Landed in New South Wales as Captain General, and Governor in Chief Of that Territory, I appointed Lieutenant George Johnson Of The Marines, to act as my Adjutant of Orders, and he continued to act as such, during the time I retained The Government.
>
> And on The Marines being relieved, His Majesty having been pleased to direct me, to raise a Company, to be annexed to The New South Wales Corps, giving The Company so raised, to The Officer Of Marines, the most Deserving, I gave that Company, to the said Lieutenant George Johnson.
>
> Being unable to appear at the late Trial, (from a Paralytic Stroke) to speak to the Conduct of Lieutenant Colonel George Johnson, whilst under my Command, I do hereby Certify, that I allways found him, during the time I retained The Government Of New South Wales, an Active, good Officer, at all times zealous, for the good of His Majesty's Service, and meriting the Confidence I placed in him.
>
> A: Phillip
>
> August the 2. 1811   Vice Admiral of The Red

Arthur Phillip. Certificate of character of Lieutenant Colonel George Johnston, 2 August 1811. SLNSW (No.93)
Phillip plainly found Johnston's character and conduct during the years of his governorship to be commendable. A paralytic stroke prevented Phillip from attending Johnston's court-martial.

I took the *Porpoise* upon the terms they had proposed for me; and the moment I got the command of the *Porpoise* I took care to keep it, and would not suffer any of their terms, or any thing which they said, to have the least influence on my mind; I took command of the ship . . . I considered myself, the moment I got on board my ship, as the legal Governor of the country, and so I considered myself to the last.[26]

He sailed in March 1809, it being thought he was sailing to England. But he sailed instead to Hobart where he hoped, vainly as it happened, to enlist the support of David Collins, the Lieutenant-Governor.

There he remained until he heard of Governor Macquarie's arrival at Sydney and he returned to Port Jackson in January 1810 though he did not return home until May.

At Rio de Janeiro in 1809 on the voyage to New South Wales with her husband, Elizabeth Macquarie heard at first hand of the events of 26 January 1808. She wrote in her diary:

Bligh Family Tombstone, Lambeth Churchyard, London. SLNSW (No.106)
The inscription on the Tombstone reads: "Sacred to the memory of William Bligh Esquire F.R.S., Vice-Admiral of the Blue the celebrated Navigator who first transplanted the Bread Fruit Tree from Otahiete to the West Indies, bravely fought the battles of his country and died beloved, respected and lamented on the 7th day of December 1871, aged 64".
There is no mention of his Governorship of New South Wales.

We had a good deal of conversation with Dr. Jamison regarding the extraordinary events which had taken place in New South Wales, and it appeared to us that *even by their own account* the conduct of those persons who had acted against the Govt. was not to be justified or even excused; we felt sorry that a man such as Col. Johnson [sic] was described to us should have committed himself as he has done, by an act of the most open and daring rebellion, by which in as far as it appears to us, he will probably forfeit a life.[27]

Macarthur and Johnston sailed to England in order to present their defence. In the event, Johnston was court-martialled and cashiered in June 1811 and returned to New South Wales to civilian life as a farmer. He died in 1823.

Macarthur being a civilian could not be tried for treason in England. Macquarie had received instructions to place him on trial if he returned to the colony. This meant exile for him until 1817 when he received permission to return providing he took no part in public affairs. He died in 1834.

After Johnston's court-martial, Bligh received regulation promotions to Rear-Admiral of the White and Vice-Admiral of the Blue. He received a pension in 1813 and died in 1817.

The overthrow of Bligh came to be called the "Rum Rebellion" though it was not caused by Bligh's attempt to control the use of rum as barter or to stop the monopoly trading of the officers. By 1808 the officers were in competition with traders like Robert Campbell and John Macarthur realized that the days of monopoly trading were over. The phrase was not used by contemporaries; it was first used 50 years after the event and reflects the concerns of that period as much as an understanding of the events of 1808.[28]

The rebellion was caused by the confrontation between two men: William Bligh and John Macarthur. Both were resolute and both were convinced of their own rectitude. Macarthur saw Bligh as the obstacle to the realization of his vision for the Australian wool industry — a vision which included a central and lucrative role for himself. Bligh, influenced by his patron, Banks, saw Macarthur as an enemy of government who had vanquished his predecessors and who must be brought under control.

Paul Brunton is Curator of Manuscripts, Mitchell Library, State Library of New South Wales.

REFERENCES

1. Philip Gidley King Letter to Under-Secretary King, 8 November 1801. Colonial Office C.O.201/20 pp.177-180. Original in Public Record Office, London. Microfilm copy held by Mitchell Library at PRO Reel 10.

2. Philip Gidley King Letter to John King, 5 June 1802. Colonial Office 201/21 pp.231-235. Original in Public Record Office, London. Microfilm copy held by Mitchell Library at PRO Reel 10.

3. Philip Gidley King Despatch to Lord Hobart, 9 May 1803. Colonial Office 201/26 pp.225-227. Original in Public Record Office, London. Microfilm copy held by Mitchell Library at PRO Reel 13.

4. Martin Mason Letter to Sir Joseph Banks, undated but after 26 January 1808. Copy contained within Bligh's personal papers. Mitchell Library S1/45 p.156.

5. Board of Trade 6/88. Original in Public Record Office, London. Microfilm copy held by Mitchell Library at PRO Reel 288.

6. Cited in Gavin Kennedy *Bligh* London,Duckworth,1978, pp342-343.

7. Admiralty 1/5368. Original held in Public Record Office, London. Quoted in Gavin Kennedy, *Bligh* London, Duckworth, 1978, pp.329-330.

8. William Bligh Letter to Sir Joseph Banks 7 March 1805. Original held in Alexander Turnbull Library, Wellington. Microfilm copy held by Mitchell Library at FM4/4791.

9. *HRNSW* Vol. 6 p.189.

10. Bartrum *Proceedings of a general court-martial . . . for the trial of . . . Geo Johnston . . .* London, Sherwood, Neely and Jones, 1811 pp.178-179

11. *Ibid* p.179.

12. Elizabeth Macarthur Letter to Miss Kingdon, 29 January 1807. Mitchell Library A2908.

13. John Blaxland Letter to an unknown correspondent, 16 October 1807 *HRNSW* Vol. 6, pp.308-12.

14. William Minchin Letter to Philip Gidley King, 20 October 1807. Mitchell Library Z ML MSS 681/2 pp.397-399.

15. John Harris Letter to Anna Josepha King, 25 October 1807 Mitchell Library A1980 pp.237-248.

16. Elizabeth Macarthur Letter to Miss Kingdon, 21 October 1807. Mitchell Library Z A2908, p.41.

17. Duke of York Letter to Viscount Castlereagh, 13 June 1808 enclosing Johnston's letter to Sir James Gordon, 8 October 1807. Colonial Office C.O.201/48 pp.245-251. Original held in Public Record Office, London. Microfilm copy held by Mitchell Library at P.R.O. Reel 24.

18. John Harris Letter to Philip Gidley King, 25 October 1807. Mitchell Library Z ML MSS 681/2 pp.401-408.

19. *HRA* 1, 6 p.312.

20. *HRA* 1, 6 p.227.

21. *Ibid*.

22. Bartrum *op cit* p.151.

23. *Ibid* pp.151-2.

24. *Ibid* p.152.

25. *HRNSW* Vol. 6 p.454.

26. Bartrum *op cit* p.33.

27. Elizabeth Macquarie Journal, 1809. Mitchell Library, Z C126, pp.41-42.

28. The first recorded use of "rum rebellion" is in William Howitt *Land, Labour and Gold*, 1855 vol. 2 p.118 according to G.A. Wilkes *A dictionary of Australian colloquialisms*, 1978 p.281.

SHIP'S COMPANY, HMS *BOUNTY*

WILLIAM BLIGH, Lieutenant (age 33): Honourably acquitted for the loss of the *Bounty*, 1790; returned to the Pacific 1791-1793; fought in the Battles of Camperdown, 1797 and Copenhagen 1801; Captain General and Governor-in-Chief of the Territory of New South Wales and its dependencies, 1806-1808 (deposed); Vice-Admiral of the Blue, 1814; died 1817.

JOHN FRYER, Master (age 33): Survived the launch voyage; continued as master in the R.N., died 1817.

WILLIAM COLE, Boatswain: Survived the launch voyage; returned to England.

WILLIAM PECKOVER, Gunner: Survived the launch voyage; returned to England.

WILLIAM PURCELL, Carpenter: Survived the launch voyage; returned to England; died in 1834, the last survivor of the crew of HMS *Bounty*.

THOMAS HUGGAN, Surgeon: Died of alcoholism in Tahiti, 8 Dec. 1788.

THOMAS LEDWARD, Surgeon's mate: Survived the launch voyage; drowned on the voyage back to the Cape in the *Welfare*.

WILLIAM ELPHINSTON, Master's mate (age 36); Survived the launch voyage; died in Batavia c.16 Oct. 1789.

FLETCHER CHRISTIAN, Master's mate, promoted Acting Lieutenant (age 22): Leader of the mutiny; settled on Pitcairn Island; probably murdered, 1793.

JOHN HALLET, Midshipman (age 15): Survived the launch voyage; returned to Tahiti in search of the mutineers in HMS *Pandora* 23 Mar. 1791; afterwards Lieutenant HMS *Penelope*, lost at sea.

PETER HEYWOOD, Midshipman (age 15): Captured at Tahiti; found guilty of mutiny but recommended for Royal Pardon; granted Oct. 1792.

THOMAS HAYWARD, Midshipman (age 20): Survived the launch voyage; returned to Tahiti in search of the mutineers in HMS *Pandora*; rose to Commander, R.N., drowned while in command of HM Sloop *Swift*.

EDWARD YOUNG, Midshipman (age 21): Settled on Pitcairn Island with fellow mutineers; thought to have died of asthma c.1800.

GEORGE STEWART, Midshipman, promoted Acting Master's mate (age 21): Captured at Tahiti; drowned in

wreck of HMS *Pandora*, on voyage back to England 28 Aug. 1791.

ROBERT TINKLER, Midshipman (age 17): Survived the launch voyage; returned to England, rose to the rank of Commander, R.N.

JOHN NORTON, Quartermaster (age 34): Killed by the Tongans off Tofoa at the beginning of the launch voyage, 3 May 1789.

PETER LINKLETTER, Quartermaster (age 30): Survived the launch voyage; died in Batavia c.16 Oct. 1789.

GEORGE SIMPSON, Quartermaster's mate (age 27); Survived the launch voyage; returned to England.

JAMES MORRISON, Boatswain's mate (age 27): Captured at Tahiti; found guilty of mutiny but recommended for a Royal Pardon; granted Oct. 1792; Gunner, R.N., died 1807.

JOHN MILLS, Gunner's mate (age 39): Settled on Pitcairn Island with fellow mutineers and murdered, 1793.

CHARLES NORMAN, Carpenter's mate (age 24); Captured at Tahiti; acquitted of mutiny, 18 Sep. 1792.

THOMAS McINTOSH, Carpenter's mate (age 25): Captured at Tahiti; acquitted of mutiny, 18 Sep. 1792.

LAWRENCE LEBOGUE, Sailmaker (age 40): Survived the launch voyage; returned to the Pacific with Bligh, 1791-1793.

JOSEPH COLEMAN, Armourer (age 36): Captured at Tahiti; acquitted of mutiny, 18 Sep. 1792.

CHARLES CHURCHILL, Corporal (age 28): Returned to Tahiti with fellow mutineers; murdered c.1790.

HENRY HILLBRANT, Cooper (age 24): Captured at Tahiti; drowned in wreck of HMS *Pandora*, on voyage back to England 28 Aug. 1791.

WILLIAM MUSPRAT, Steward (age 27): Captured at Tahiti; found guilty of mutiny but discharged on a legal technicality.

JOHN SAMUEL, Clerk (age 26): Survived the launch voyage; continued in the R.N., rose to paymaster.

THOMAS HALL, Cook (age 38): Survived the launch voyage; died in Batavia, 11 Oct. 1789.

JOHN SMITH, Commander's Cook (age 36): Survived the launch voyage; returned with Bligh to the Pacific, 1791-1793.

ROBERT LAMB, Butcher (age 21): Survived the launch voyage; died on the voyage back to England.

RICHARD SKINNER, Able Seaman (age 22): Captured at Tahiti; drowned in wreck of HMS *Pandora*, on voyage back to England 28 Aug. 1791.

ALEXANDER SMITH (true name, JOHN ADAMS), Able Seaman (age 20): Settled on Pitcairn Island with fellow mutineers; last surviving mutineer on Pitcairn Island; died 5 Mar. 1829.

THOMAS BURKITT, Able Seaman (age 25): Captured at Tahiti; found guilty of mutiny and desertion; hanged on board HMS *Brunswick*, 29 Oct. 1792.

JOHN MILLWARD, Able Seaman (age 21): Captured at Tahiti; found guilty of mutiny and desertion; hanged on board HMS *Brunswick*, 29 Oct. 1792.

JOHN WILLIAMS, Able Seaman (age 26): Settled on Pitcairn Island with fellow mutineers; murdered 1792.

JOHN SUMNER, Able Seaman (age 22): Captured at Tahiti; drowned in wreck of HMS *Pandora*, on voyage back to England 28 Aug. 1792.

MATTHEW THOMPSON, Able Seaman (age 37): Returned to Tahiti with fellow mutineers; murdered 1790. JAMES VALENTINE, Able Seaman (age 28): Died of blood poisoning aboard HMS *Bounty*, 9 Oct. 1788.

MICHAEL BYRNE, Able Seaman Captured at Tahiti; acquitted of mutiny, 18 Sep. 1792.

WILLIAM McCOY, Able Seaman (age 23): Settled on Pitcairn Island with fellow mutineers; fell from a cliff while drunk, 1799.

MATTHEW QUINTAL, Able Seaman (age 21): An American from Philadelphia; settled on Pitcairn Island with fellow mutineers; murdered 1799.

ISAAC MARTIN, Able Seaman (age 30): Settled on Pitcairn Island with fellow mutineers; murdered 1793.

THOMAS ELLISON, Able Seaman (age 19): Captured at Tahiti; found guilty of mutiny and desertion; hanged on board HMS *Brunswick*, 29 Oct. 1792.

DAVID NELSON, Gardener/Botanist appointed by Sir Joseph Banks: Survived the launch voyage; died at Coupang, Timor 18 July 1789.

WILLIAM BROWN, Gardener/Botanist's assistant (age 25): Settled on Pitcairn Island with fellow mutineers; murdered, 1793.

CATALOGUE OF EXHIBITION ITEMS

WILLIAM BLIGH AND THE GEORGIAN NAVY

1. Henry Roberts. Matavai Bay, Tahiti, 1773. Pen, ink and wash drawing. 32.4 × 56.5 cm. ML ZPXD 11, f.13

1. Henry Roberts. Ulietea, one of the Society Islands, 1773? Wash drawing, 30.8 × 54 cm. ML ZPXD 11, f.23

1. Henry Roberts. Huaheine, one of the Society Islands, 1773? Wash drawing, 35.9 × 53.7 cm. ML ZPXD 11, f.22

2. William Hodges. The Otaheite Fleet at Appany Bay, 1774.
Pen and wash drawing, 36.8 × 54 cm. ML ZPXD 11, f.14

2. William Hodges. War Canoe, Otaheite, 1774. Wash drawing, 36.8 × 54.9 cm. ML ZPXD 11, f.15

2. William Hodges. Canoes, Otaheite, 1774? Wash drawing, 27 × 40 cm. ML ZPXD 11, f.15a

3. John Webber (attrib.) William Bligh, c.1776. Oil, 62.2 × 74.3 cm. Private collection, United Kingdom

4. John Webber. Elizabeth Bligh, 1782. Oil, 61 × 71.1 cm. Private collection, United Kingdom

5. James Burney. 'Journal' kept on HM Sloop Discovery, 1776-1779. Original autograph manuscript. ML Z Safe 1/64

6. William Bligh. Letter to James Burney, 26 July, 1791. Original autograph manuscript. DL ZMSQ 163, pp.6-7

7. William Hodges. View of part of Oaitepeha Bay in the Islands of Otahiti, 1773. Oil, 33 × 51 cm. National Maritime Museum, London BHC 1937

8. William Hodges. Owharee Harbour, Huaheine, 1773. Oil, 33 × 51 cm. National Maritime Museum, London BHC 1840

9. William Hodges. View of the Island of Otaha and Bola Bola with part of the Island of Ulietea, 1773-1774. Oil, 34.5 × 51.5 cm. National Maritime Museum, London BHC 2376

SIR JOSEPH BANKS AND THE COMMERCIAL EXPLOITATION OF THE BREADFRUIT

10. *Banks Florilegium*
Plants from the Society Islands, Tahiti, collected by Sir Joseph Banks, drawn by Sydney Parkinson, and printed by Alecto Historical Editions, London, 1980-1990, from the plates in The Natural History Museum, London. *Cordia subcordata* (no.623); *Ipomoea littoralis* (no.630) *Ipomoea illustris* (no.631); *Solanum repandrum* (no.632) *Solanum viride* (no.633), ML

11. Thomas Phillips. Sir Joseph Banks, c.1808-1809. Oil, 141.3 × 119 cm. DG ZDG 25

12. Breadfruit Specimens (botanical names of species). Herbarium, Royal Botanic Gardens, Sydney

13. John Ellis. *A Description of the Mangostan and the Breadfruit*. London, 1775. ML Q581.63/E

FITTING OUT FOR A VOYAGE TO THE SOUTH SEAS

14. Sheer Draught of the *Bounty*, late *Bethia* of London, 25th June, 1787. Pen and ink drawing, 50.5 × 75 cm. National Maritime Museum, London 6339/66

15. M. Wilson and K. Britten. Scale model, of HM Armed Transport *Bounty*, 1989. 76(h) × 91.5(l) × 38 (w) cm.; scale 1:48. National Maritime Museum, London

16. Sir Joseph Banks, copy of a letter to Sir George Young, 7 Sept. 1787. Original autograph manuscript. ML ZA 78-4 p.20

17. George Robinson. HM Armed Transport *Bounty*, 19--. Watercolour, 24 × 32.5 cm. National Maritime Museum, London, 60 H 1727

18. Plan and profile of after part of *Bounty*'s Lower Deck, as fitted out for carrying breadfruit, May 1790. Pen and ink drawing, 30.5 × 58 cm. National Maritime Museum, London 6341/66

18. Deck plan of HMS *Bounty*, 20 November 1787. Pen and ink drawing, 51 × 75 cm. National Maritime Museum, London 6340 A

18. Deck plan of the *Bounty*, November 1787. Pen and ink drawing, 50.5 × 67 cm. National Maritime Museum, London 6340/66

19. William Buchan. *Domestic Medicine*. London, Milner, 1779. National Maritime Museum, London D6069

20. HMS *Bounty*'s chronometer, made by Larcum Kendall, London, 1771. 125 cm. (diameter). National Maritime Museum, London, K2

21. Brass telescope in mahogany case, inscribed "Capt. Wm. Bligh Royal Navy", made by Troughton, London. 69(l) × 9(w) cm. ML ZLR6

THE FIRST BREADFRUIT VOYAGE IN HMS BOUNTY

22. William Bligh. 'Log of the proceedings of His Majesty's Ship *Bounty* on a Voyage to the South Seas', 1787-1788. Original autograph manuscript. ML Z Safe 1/46

23. John Webber. Poedua, daughter of the chieftain of Raiatea, c.1785. Oil, 144.8 × 94 cm. National Library of Australia, Canberra, Rex Nan Kivell collection NK 5192

24. William Bligh. 'A Sketch from recollection and Anchor Bearings of the North part of Otaheite from Point Venus to Taownes Harbour, c.1788.' Original autograph manuscript. Ink and wash, 23 × 36.5 cm. ML ZA 78-4 p.112

25. John Webber. A Dancing Girl of Otaheite, 1777. Pencil, ink and wash drawing, with watercolour, 49.5 × 35.5 cm. DL Pe 216

25. John Webber. A Dance in Otaheite, c.1781-3. Ink, wash and watercolour drawing, 22.7 × 37.8 cm. DL ZPXX2, f.13

25. John Webber. A Young Woman of Otaheite, bringing a present, c.1781. Ink, wash and watercolour drawing, 22.5 × 18.4 cm. DL ZPXX2, f.12

THE MUTINY

26. Robert Dodd. Mutineers turning Bligh and part of the Officers and Crew adrift from His Majesty's Ship the *Bounty*, 1790? Oil, 49.5 × 68 cm. Berkelouw Book Dealers, Berrima, NSW

27. William Bligh. 'Log of the proceedings of His Majesty's Ship *Bounty* Lieut. Wm. Bligh Commander

from Otaheite towards Jamaica' 5 Apr. 1789 — 13 Mar. 1790. Original autograph manuscript. ML Z Safe 1/47

28. William Bligh. 'Rough account — Lieutenant Wm Bligh's voyage in the *Bounty*'s Launch from the ship to Tofoa and from thence to Timor —' 28 Apr. 1789 — 14 June 1789. Original autograph manuscript. National Library of Australia, Canberra MS 5393

29. William Bligh. 'Resources Sick Book', 27 July 1789 - 20 Aug. 1789. Original autograph manuscript. ML Z Safe 1/45

30. William Bligh. Description of the mutineers, compiled 14 June 1789 — 20 Aug. 1789. Original manuscript signed by W. Bligh. ML Z Safe 1/43

31. Francois Peron and Charles Lesueur. Vue de Coupang (View of Kupang), *in Voyage de decouvertes aux Terres Australes, Historique; Atlas* par M.M. Lesueur et Petit. 2nd edition. Paris, A. Bertrand, 1824. Engraving, 45.5 × 17 cm. ML F980/P, pl.37

32. Charles Benezach. Lieut. Bligh and his crew of the ship *Bounty* hospitably received by the Governor of Timor, 1791. Engraving, 24 × 38 cm. ML SV*/BLIGH/2

33. Robert Dodd. Mutineers turning Bligh and part of the Officers and Crew adrift from His Majesty's Ship the *Bounty*, 1790? Handcoloured aquatint engraving, published London, 49.5 × 68 cm. DL Pf137

34. William Bligh. Letter to his wife Elizabeth, 19 Aug. 1789. Original autograph manuscript. ML Z Safe 1/45

35. R.A. Lightly. Model of the *Bounty*'s launch, 1988. 15.5 (h) × 5.5 (w) × 15 (l) cm.; scale 1:4. National Maritime Museum, London

36. 'A Copy of the Draught from which the *Bounty*s Launch was built' from the papers of Sir Joseph Banks. Pen and ink drawing, 24 × 41.5 cm. ML ZA 78-4, p.16

37. Gaetano Calleyo. John Fryer, c.1807. Oil, 69 × 53.5 cm. ML ZML 413

38. William Bligh. *A Narrative of The Mutiny on Board His Majesty's Ship* Bounty . . . London, George Nicol, 1790. ML C695

39. William Bligh. *A Narrative of the Mutiny on Board His Majesty's Ship* Bounty . . . Dutch edition. Rotterdam, G.A. Arrenberg, 1790. ML 988/55 B1

40. John Fryer. 'Account of the seizure of His Majesty's Armed Vessel *Bounty* 28th April 1789 Jo Fryer', c. 1 Oct. 1789. Original autograph manuscript. ML Z Safe 1/38

41. Homann Heirs. Der Hollaendischen Ostindianschen Compagnie Haupt. Handels . . . Batavia [A Map of the Settlement of Batavia in the Dutch East Indies]. Nurnberg, Homann Erben, 1733, Handcoloured engraving, 65 × 80 cm. ML ZM2/478.99/ JAKARTA/1733

42. William Bligh. Letter to Duncan Campbell, 13 Oct. 1789. Original autograph manuscript. ML Z Safe 1/40

43. William Bligh. Report to Sir Joseph Banks of the mutiny on H.M.S. *Bounty*, 13 Oct. 1789. Original manuscript annotated and signed by W. Bligh. ML Z Safe 1/36

44. William Bligh. Letter to Sir Joseph Banks, 13 Oct. 1789. Original autograph manuscript. ML ZA 78-4, pp.104-107

HMS *PANDORA* IN PURSUIT OF THE MUTINEERS

45. Admiralty Records. Captain Edwards Memorandum made at Tahiti, 1791. Original manuscript. Public Record Office, London PRO/ADMI/1763

46. James Morrison. Journal, compiled c.25 Nov. 1792 + Original autograph manuscript with annotations in another hand, possibly Peter Heywood. ML Z Safe 1/42

47. Artefacts from the wreck of the *Pandora*, 1791. Various items. Queensland Museum, Brisbane

48. Admiralty Records. Enquiry into the loss of HMS *Pandora*, 1792. Original manuscript. Public Record Office, London PRO/ADM 1/5330 pt.2

49. Robert Batty, after Peter Heywood. H.M. Ship *Pandora* in the act of foundering. Proof engraving later issued in John Barrow, *The Eventful History of the Mutiny and Piratical Seizure of HMS* Bounty (1831), 10.7 × 15.3 cm. DG SV8.1, no.13

50. A New Chart of the Eastern Coast of New Holland from South Cape to Cape York. London, Laurie and Whittle, 1798 (i.e. c.1800). Engraving, 105 × 68 cm. ML ZM4/804/1799/1

COURT MARTIAL OF THE *BOUNTY* MUTINEERS

51. Peter Heywood. Letter to his mother from Batavia, 20 Nov. 1791. Original autograph manuscript. National Maritime Museum, London MS 78/184.

52. John Simpson. Captain Peter Heywood, 1812-1825? Oil, 76 × 63.5 cm. National Maritime Museum, London BHC 2766

53. James Morrison. Memorandum and letter to Rev. William Howell, 10 Oct. 1792. Original autograph manuscript. ML Z Safe 1/33

54. William Bligh. 'Rems [i.e. Remarks] on Court Martial' 18 Sep. 1792 + Original autograph manuscript. ML Z Safe 1/43

55. Peter Heywood. Letter to Dr. Scott from HMS *Hector*, 20 Sept. 1792. Original autograph manuscript. National Maritime Museum, London MS 78/184

56. William Bligh. Notes on Edward Christian's letters to Sir Joseph Banks, c. Dec. 1792. Original autograph manuscript. ML Z Safe 1/43

57. Stephen Barney *Minutes of the proceedings of the court-martial held at Portsmouth, August 12, 1792, on ten persons charged with mutiny on board His Majesty's Ship the* Bounty. London, J. Deighton, 1794. DL 79/15

58. William Bligh. Letter to his nephew, Francis Godolphin Bond, 26 July 1794. Original autograph manuscript. National Maritime Museum, London BND 1-35

59. William Bligh. *An Answer to Certain Assertions* . . . London, G. Nichol, 1794. ML C839

THE HISTORY OF THE PITCAIRNERS

60. Soundscape: Language of the Mutineers; Tapes of the dialect spoken on Norfolk Island. Norfolk Island Museum

61. Sheathing nail from HMS *Bounty*, recovered from the wreck, 1957. ML Pic. Acc. 5782

62. Richard Beechey. View of Watering Place at Gambier's Islands, 1826. Watercolour, 18.7 × 292 cm. DG SV8.1/2

63. George Dashwood. View in Pitcaine's [sic] Island, 1833. Watercolour, 23.5 × 16.9 cm. ML ZPXA 1679, f.58b

64. Richard Beechey (*attrib*). Landing at Bounty Bay, c.1825. Oil, 75.3 × 11.3 cm. ML ZML 114.

65. Richard Beechey. John Adams, 1825? Pencil and ink drawing, 21 × 17 cm. (approx.) ML P2/82

66. John Adams? Narrative of the mutiny on HMS *Bounty* given to Captain Beechey, December 1825. Original manuscript signed by John Adams. ML A 1804

67. John Adams' Pigtail. National Maritime Museum, London RUSI 526

67. John Adams' Sea Chest. 36 × 93 × 41 cm. National Maritime Museum, London RUSI 1216

67. Pitcairn Island Prayer Book. 17 × 21 cm. National Maritime Museum, London RUSI 524

67. Tombstone from the grave of John Adams (d.1829), originally on Pitcairn Island. Lead-covered wooden board, 69 × 36 cm. National Maritime Museum, London W73-49

68. Frederick William Beechey. *Narrative of a Voyage to the Pacific* by Capt. F.W. Beechey . . . London, Henry Colburn and Richard Bentley, 1831 ML Q980/B

69. Henry Hutchinson Montgomery. Portrait of Mrs Sarah Nobbs (nee Christian), widow of Rev. G.H. Nobbs, 1893-1896. Reproduction of original photographic print, 14.7 × 10 cm. ML PXA 445, no.36

70. Rev. George Hunn Nobbs 'The Pitcairn Island Recorder', 1 Jan. 1838 — 31 May 1838. Original autograph manuscript. ML ZC134

71. Robert Batty, after William Smyth. Residence of John Adams, Pitcairn Island. Proof engraving later issued in John Barrow. *The Eventful History of the Mutiny and Piratical Seizure of HMS* Bounty, (1831), 10.7 × 15.3 cm. DG SV8.1, no.14

71. Robert Batty, after William Smyth. George Young and his wife. Proof engraving later issued in Barrow (1831), 10.7 × 15.3 cm. DG SV8.1, no.15

72. John Eyre. A View of Queenborough on Norfolk Island, 1801-1804? Watercolour, 19.9 × 33.3 cm. (inside frame lines). ML ZSV8/NORF I/2

72. John Eyre. Phillipsburg, Norfolk Island, 1801-1804? Watercolour, 19.5 × 30.5 cm. ML ZSV8/NORF I/3

72. John Eyre. A View of Sydney, Norfolk Island, 1801-1804? Watercolour, 24.5 × 42.8 cm. (inside frame lines). ML ZSV8/NORF I/1

73. Photographs taken on Pitcairn Island by the crew of HMS *Cambrian*, 1905-1907. Reproductions of original prints, 10.5 × 15.5 cm. ML PXB 2, ff.24, 25, 26

74. E. Were. Photographs taken on Pitcairn Island, 1930s. Reproductions of original photographic prints, 14.9 × 21.1 cm. Lent for copying by E. Were, 1965. ML Pic. Acc. 729

75. Photographs taken of Pitcairn Islanders by a crew member (C.B.C.) of HMS *Pelorus*, c.1860-1862. Reproductions of original prints, 14.7 × 20.1 cm. ML Q 980/C, ff.26, 27, 28

76. Portrait of George Parkyn Christian (1853-1940), great-grandson of Fletcher Christian, c.1930-1940. Reproduction of original photographic print, 21.5 × 16.5 cm. ML P1/Christian

77. Rev. George Hunn Nobbs' land grant for Norfolk Island, 14 Sep. 1859. Original manuscript on vellum form. ML MSS 3886/2 Item 1

78. The Holy Bible. Cambridge, Society for Promoting Christian Knowledge, 18 --. With presentation inscription. DL 8/22

79. The Norfolk Island Pioneer, 26 Nov. 1885. ML A 2881-12, pp.87-90

GOVERNOR BLIGH IN NEW SOUTH WALES

80. Marc Clark. Maquette for Statue of William Bligh erected on Circular Quay West, 1987. Bronze, 16 × 36 × 10 cm. David McNicoll, Sydney

81. George William Evans (*attrib*.) Government House, Parramatta, 1808-1809? SLNSW

81. George William Evans (*attrib*.) Government House, Sydney, 1808-1809? SLNSW

81. George William Evans (*attrib*.) The Settlement on the Green Hills [Windsor] Hawksburgh [sic] River, N.S.Wales, 1809. Watercolour, 23.8 × 36.7 cm. ML ZPXD 388, v.3, f.7

81. Artist unknown. Government Agricultural Establishment, Castle Hill, 1806? Watercolour, 24 × 35 cm. ML ZPX*D 379 v.1, f.9

81. George William Evans (*attrib*.) Sydney Cove, West Side, 1810. Watercolour, 32 × 47 cm. ML ZML 47

81. John William Lewin. Sydney Cove, 1808. Watercolour, 28 × 53 cm. ML ZML 50

82. Lord Camden. Letter to Sir Joseph Banks, 18 Apr. 1805. Original manuscript. ML ZA 84, pp.23-26

83. William Bligh. Letter to Sir Joseph Banks, 25 Apr. 1805. Original autograph manuscript. ML ZA 84, p.37

84. Artist unknown. Miniature portrait of William Bligh, 1814? Watercolour on ivory, 60 × 51 cm. ML Z Min 53

85. Artist unknown. Miniature portrait of Mary Putland (nee Bligh), daughter of William and Elizabeth Bligh, c.1800. Watercolour on ivory, 67 × 54 cm. DG Min 2

86. Mary Putland. Letter to her sisters, Harriet, Betsey, Fanny, Jane and Anne Bligh, 26 Feb. 1806 to 15 Mar. 1806. Original autograph manuscript. ML Z Safe 1/45

87. Charles Lesueur. Plan de la ville de Sydney, Capitale des Colonies Anglaises aux Terres Australes . . . 1802 (Plan of the town of Sydney, capital of the English colonies in Australia *in Voyage de decouvertes aux Terres Australes . . . Historique Atlas* Paris, 1824. Engraving, 15.2 × 21.3 cm. ML F 980/P, pl.17

88. Robert Dighton. Lieutenant-Colonel George Johnston. 1810. Watercolour, 54.6 × 39.4 cm. ML ZML 511

89. Henry Smith Robinson, after Robert Dighton. Lieutenant-Colonel George Johnston, 1853. Oil, 109.8 × 83.9 cm. ML ZML 9

90. George Johnston. Commission as major to the New South Wales Corps, 13 November 1810. Printed form completed in manuscript on vellum. DL MSQ22, Item 17a

91. George Johnston. Copy of letter to Lord Liverpool, 16 November 1810. DL MSQ22, Item 19

92. D'Arcy Wentworth. Letter to Lord Fitzwilliam, 17 October 1807. Original autograph manuscript. DL MSQ22, Item 59

93. Arthur Phillip. Certificate of character of Lieutenant-Colonel George Johnston, 2 August 1811. Original manuscript signed by A. Phillip. DL MSQ22, Item 55

94. John Macarthur. Letter to Elizabeth Macarthur, 1808. Original autograph manuscript. ML ZA 2898

95. Edward Abbott. Letter to Captain Philip Gidley King, 13 Feb. 1808. Original autograph manuscript. ML ZA 1976

96. Artist unknown. Arrest of Governor Bligh, 1808. Watercolour, 23.3 × 37 cm. ML Z Safe 4/5 Arrest of Governor Bligh, 1808. Lithograph of original watercolour, published by NSW Government Printing Office, Sydney, c.1890. ML A 1982

97. Officers and settlers of New South Wales. Requisition to Major Johnston to assume control of the colony and to arrest Governor Bligh, 1808. Original manuscript. ML Z Safe 4/5

98. Free settlers and cultivators of N.S.W. memorial to Viscount Castlereagh, 3 Nov. 1808. Original manuscript. ML A660/1

99. William Bligh. Account of the Rebellion, 30 Jan. 1808. Original manuscript. ML ZA 78-5

BLIGH RELICS

100. Dress Sword of William Bligh. Date unknown. 84 × 11.6 cm. Nickel plated steel with bronze grip. DL DR 107

101. Sword believed to have been captured from Admiral de Winter, Battle of Camperdown, 1797, made by S. Brunn, London. 91 × 12.5 cm. (approx.) ML ZLR 5

102. Signet ring and seal of William Bligh. Date unknown. Layered chalcedony in gold; carnelian in gold. DL DR 188a, b

103. Wax impression from William Bligh's private seal. Red sealing wax. ML ZR 241d

104. Bligh Family bible, 1611. ML A 2049

105. William Bligh. Last will and testament, 1818, from the records of Norton Smith & Co. Original manuscript on vellum form. ML A 5434-1, Item 1

106. Bligh Family tombstone, Lambeth Churchyard, London. Print from original glass negative. ML GN 11, box 7, no.91

BOUNTY MYTHS

107. Theatre Royal, Drury Lane, London. *Playbill: Pitcairn's Island, A Romantick Operatick Ballet Spectacle founded on the Recent Discovery of a numerous Colony formed by and descended from the Mutineers of the* Bounty *Frigate*. London, Lowndes, Printer, 1816. ML 792.5/T

108. George Gordon, Lord Byron. *The Island, or Christian and his Comrades*. London, John Hunt, 1823. DL 82/86

109. John Marshall. *Royal Naval Biography* . . . vol.II. part II, London, Longman, Hurst, Rees, Orme, Brown and Green, 1825. GRL DS 359.0942/128

110. John Barrow, editor. *The Eventful History of the Mutiny and Piratical Seizure of H.M.S.* Bounty: *its Cause and Consequences*. London, John Murray, 1831. DL 83/95

111. Lady Diana Belcher. *The Mutineers of the* Bounty *and their Descendants in Pitcairn and Norfolk Islands*. London, John Murray, 1870. ML 999.7/B

112. Raymond Hollis Longford, director and producer. *The Mutiny of the* Bounty, 1917. Silent film stills and poster. National Film and Sound Archive, Canberra

113. Charles Chauvel, director and producer. *In the Wake of the* Bounty, 1933. Film stills. National Film and Sound Archive, Canberra

114. Frank Lloyd, director and Irving Thalberg, producer. *Mutiny on the* Bounty, 1935. M.G.M. film stills. National Film and Sound Archive, Canberra and National Maritime Museum, London. Courtesy M.G.M.

115. Lewis Milestone, director. *Mutiny on the* Bounty, 1962, M.G.M. film stills. National Film and Sound Archive, Canberra and National Maritime Museum, London. Courtesy M.G.M.

116. Roger Donaldson, director. *The* Bounty, 1984. Columbia/EM1/Warner film stills and poster. National Film and Sound Archive, Canberra and National Maritime Museum, London. Courtesy M.G.M.

BLIGH'S SECOND BREADFRUIT VOYAGE IN HMS *PROVIDENCE* AND THE TENDER ASSISTANT, 1791-1793

117. Artist unknown. Nathaniel Portlock. Oil, 76 × 63.5 cm. National Maritime Museum, London

118. George Tobin. Album of sketches on HMS *Providence*, 1791-1793. Watercolours, 18.1 × 26.3 cm. (or approx.) ML ZPXA 563

119. George Tobin. Journal of H.M.S. *Providence*, Aug. 1791 — Jan. 1793. Original autograph manuscript. ML ZA 562

120. William Bligh. Log of HMS *Providence*, July 1791 — Sept. 1793. Original autograph manuscript. ML ZA 564 -1, -2.

121. William Bligh and George Holwell. Album of sketches on HMS *Providence*, 1791-1793. Watercolours, 29.7 × 19.4 cm. (or approx.) ML ZPXA 565

122. William Bligh, Matthew Flinders, George Holwell. Charts for the voyage of H.M.S. *Providence*. 1789-1800. Original manuscript charts. 54 × 137.5 cm. DL Safe

123. Thomas Gosse. Transplanting of the Bread-fruit-trees from Otaheite, 1796. Hand coloured mezzotint, published London, 49.5 × 60.5 cm. DL Pf 86

Collections of the State Library of New South Wales

DG Dixson Galleries
DL Dixson Library
GRL General Reference Library
ML Mitchell Library

The number in parentheses appearing at the end of all captions for illustrations refers to the item number in the Catalogue of Exhibition Items.

FURTHER READING

The best biographies of William Bligh are Gavin Kennedy *Bligh* London, Duckworth, 1978, revised and reprinted 1989 and George Mackaness *The Life of Vice-Admiral William Bligh*, R.N., F.R.S. 2 vols. Sydney, Angus & Robertson, 1931.

Many of the documents relating to the mutiny have been published in *A book of the Bounty* edited by George Mackaness with an introduction by Gavin Kennedy. London, Dent, 1981. Everyman's Library.

Three letters written by William Bligh following the mutiny to his wife, Betsy, to Duncan Campbell and Sir Joseph Banks, have been published in facsimile with transcriptions. The letters are held by the Mitchell Library, State Library of New South Wales, and were published by the Library in association with Allen and Unwin in *Awake, Bold Bligh*, edited by Paul Brunton, 1989.

Bligh's own account of the mutiny was published in 1790: *A narrative of the mutiny on board His Majesty's ship Bounty* . . . London, G. Nicol. A modern edition was published in 1981 edited by Robert Bowman (Gloucester, Alan Sutton Publishing).

Bligh's account of the *Bounty* voyage, which incorporated his 1790 account of the mutiny, was published in 1792: *A voyage to the South Seas* . . . London, G. Nicol. A modern facsimile edition was published in 1969 (Adelaide, Libraries Board of South Australia).

Bligh's private log of the *Bounty* voyage, held in the Mitchell Library, State Library of New South Wales, has not been published. The copy of this which was made by Bligh's clerk for presentation to the Admiralty, which varies from the private log, has been published in both facsimile and transcription. A transcription was published in 1937 by Golden Cockerel Press, London with an introduction by Owen Rutter. A facsimile edition was published in 1975 by Genesis Publications, Guildford, England.

The notebook which Bligh used while in the launch and which is now in the National Library of Australia has been published in both facsimile and transcription edited by John Bach (Allen & Unwin in association with the National Library of Australia 1987).

The journals of James Morrison and John Fryer, both of which are held in the Mitchell Library, State Library of New South Wales, and both of which were written after the event, have been published in transcription. Morrison's journal was published in 1935 (London, Golden Cockerel Press,) and Fryer's was published in 1934 (*Voyage of the Bounty's launch* . . . London, Golden Cockerel Press). Both books were edited by Owen Rutter.